the dance of restoration

Abel Ortega and Melodie Fleming

D1598917

REBUILDING MARRIAGE AFTER INFIDELITY

*the dance
of restoration*

Abel Ortega and Melodie Fleming

LIVING
INK
BOOKS
Writing Worth Reading

The Dance of Restoration: Rebuilding Marriage after Infidelity
Copyright © 2005 by Melodie Fleming and Abel Ortega
Published by Living Ink Books, an imprint of AMG Publishers
6815 Shallowford Rd.
Chattanooga, Tennessee 37421

ISBN 0-89957-127-1

First printing—April 2005

Cover designed by Daryle Beam, Market Street Design, Inc.,
    Chattanooga, Tennessee
Interior design and typesetting by Reider Publishing Services,
    West Hollywood, California
Edited and Proofread by Karen Brunson, Christy Phillippe,
    Dan Penwell, Sharon Neal, and Rick Steele

Printed in Canada
10 09 08 07 06 05 –T– 8 7 6 5 4 3 2 1

To my dear wife Rachel.
Thank you for your love, support, and undying
faithfulness these 41 years.
My love for you grows sweeter with the passing of each.

—ABEL

To my husband Tom.
Your encouragement and support means more to
me than I can adequately express. And your love,
faithfulness, and tenderness make me a better
person every day. I am proud to bear your name.

—MELODIE

Acknowledgments

We would like to express our gratitude to the following:

Our Lord and Savior Jesus Christ, who is our Hope and Purpose. Because He lives, each day brings new mercies.

Teal Mandl for your expert advice and Cindy Grimes for your capable assistance.

The secretaries, support staff, and volunteers of Ortega and Associates and Baptist Temple Church for your many errands and odd jobs that helped us produce this book.

"Aunt Lindsey" and all the other great babysitters who entertained Melodie's son, Matthew.

The congregations of Trinity Baptist Church and Baptist Temple Church of McAllen, Texas, who prayed for and supported us throughout this process.

ACKNOWLEDGMENTS

To our families who patiently waited and encouraged us while we spent time away from them to produce this book.

Moonbeans Coffee Shop, The Bean Bag Coffee Depot, the Millennium Restaurant, and the Junction Café, all of whom served up great coffee and allowed Melodie to sit for hours while working on the manuscript. And to the libraries of Hidalgo County, Texas, who provided quiet places to labor.

To our agent Les Stobbe who held our hands and helped us through the process.

And to Dan Penwell whose encouragement meant more than he'll ever know.

Contents

Introduction

Adultery devastates marriage. When two people are trying to overcome the destruction it brings, the task can seem overwhelming. But there is hope. The Lord of the universe is the author of love and sexuality. He ordained marriage, and He will gladly lend His almighty hand to aid in restoration. Yet, He never promises to provide an easy path. Most of the life's lessons are learned through struggle. Rebuilding a marriage after infidelity usually proves to be among the greatest of those struggles.

The fact that you are reading these words right now indicates that you care about marriage. You have probably witnessed firsthand the incredible pain that results when a spouse is unfaithful. Be encouraged. There is help.

This book was written for two groups of people. First, it was written for couples who are attempting to rebuild a marital relationship after betrayal has robbed it of trust. Within these pages, husbands and wives will learn what obstacles they can expect to encounter on the path toward healing and will find practical help for overcoming those obstacles. We've intentionally kept the book short and simple because we know how difficult it is to read while under great stress. We've also written a story that runs throughout the course of the book and helps to illustrate the instructional points.

People who love and counsel these hurting couples comprise the other group who will benefit from this book. Interspersed throughout the text and footnotes are principles designed specifically to help those who are walking the path of restoration alongside the wounded couple. Pastors and counselors, especially, have been in the forefront of our minds as we have written these helps.

We've organized our thoughts in simple fashion in order to make them easy to read. However, relationships—especially those in crisis—are not known for their simplicity but for their complexity. If you are struggling and in great pain, we recommend that you skip to the chapter that most applies to your current situation in order to bring relief. However, remember that in doing this, you are simply applying first aid to the wound. It is important that you go back to the beginning as soon as possible in order to gain an understanding of the complete process. This is especially true if you are the spouse who has been unfaithful. You are the partner who is charged with the difficult task of accepting a great amount of anger aimed in your direction. Rebuilding the marriage requires that you deal with this anger in an understanding manner. Reading through the concepts in the following pages will help you to attain the understanding that will be required for this task. The wounded spouse, on the other hand, will find this book to be a source of strength and protection.

It is our sincere prayer that the advice that follows will become a tool in the hands of our loving Father. May God bless the rebuilding of your marriage as you enter the restoration process.

Suspicions

"Are you having an affair?"

"What kind of question is that?" Robert looked surprised.

"An honest one," replied Joyce. For months she had noticed the signs. He was staying at the office later and later. She had seen Teresa's car in the company parking lot that weekend he'd been sent to New England. Why hadn't he mentioned that Teresa had been sent on the trip, as well? At home he was moody—one minute, affectionate; the next, withdrawn. And then there was the earring. She'd found it in the car last night. At first she asked about it innocently, but he was too nonchalant, too eager to explain.

"Oh, that's Teresa's," he had said. "I took her home one night when her car wouldn't start. Poor thing. We worked so hard on the Benson account. She fell asleep with her head against the window. Guess it must have slipped off while she was sleeping."

"Oh." That's all she said. Just, "Oh." Never mind that the earring had been found on the opposite side of the seat. Never mind his sudden change of subject, his rambling on about other things. *He never talks to me like this*, she thought. *Never. I usually can't get two words out of him. Now, suddenly it's 'Darling' this and 'Sweetheart' that."*

Awkwardly he turned the conversation back to the earring.

"Here," he said. "Let me take the earring to the office tomorrow for Teresa—uh—assuming, of course, that it's hers. It doesn't belong to one of your friends from church, does it?" By then, she was numb. She knew. Without replying, she handed him the earring. There was a slight tremor in his hand as he accepted it. Their eyes met. There was no mistaking the look on his face. He shifted his gaze back to the road, and again he began rambling about everything from his favorite pizza topping to his opinions about his firm's latest business moves. Normally, she would have basked in such attentiveness. But she knew it was just a cover for the truth. Even so, she stayed silent. She would give herself the night to think it through. Perhaps she was being too hasty. She couldn't make her heart accept what her instincts were telling her.

And now here he stood, shaving, as though she had simply asked him what he wanted for breakfast. She had dropped a bombshell, and he had barely winced.

"I asked you a question," she said. She had stayed awake most of the night trying to find the courage to confront him. She wasn't about to let him ignore her now.

"What?"

"Are you having an affair?"

Half of his face was covered in shaving cream. He paused, and looked straight at her. "No," he said, "I am not having an affair."

The moment felt like it was happening in slow motion.

"Oh," she said it again, and she hated herself for it. She wanted to scream and throw things at him. She wanted to explode with rage, to slap him and hurt him and make him tell her the truth. But she also wanted to believe him. Paralyzed by his nonchalant response, "Oh" was all she said. Robert resumed shaving. "Don't be so suspicious," he said. "You always think the worst of me." She went downstairs to prepare breakfast before they left for church.

~

Joyce and Robert are not real people, but their story is typical of the thousands of cases that are uncovered in counseling offices across the country. Adultery is more common than many people realize. At least 50 percent of most therapeutic caseloads are related to marriage counseling. Many of these cases involve some form of adultery.

In our story, Joyce noticed that things were not right in her marriage well before she was certain that Robert was having an affair. Many things were occurring that made her suspicious. Communication had broken down. Silence had taken its place. Teresa's car was with Robert's at an unexplained time. Robert had been coming home late from work.

Suspicions about an affair often occur well before the proof is evident.[1] Changes in behavior and emotions are noticed. In some cases, the cheating spouse vacillates between increased affection and complete withdrawal. Sometimes friendliness and warmth disappear from the relationship altogether.

Quite often, the sexual relationship within the marriage changes. In some cases, the frequency is altered. In others, the frequency remains the same, but subtle differences during love-making can be noticed.

After a while, more concrete clues begin to emerge. The faithful spouse discovers unexplained receipts for romantic gifts and credit-card charges from unfamiliar hotels. The phone is answered, but the caller hangs up quickly. The suspected spouse repeatedly steps outside when taking phone calls. Unusual charges appear on the cell-phone bill. Odd items are missing from the home, such as jewelry, lingerie, or cologne. The suspected spouse alters his or her manner of dress. Unusual attentiveness is shown to a particular person at parties or church socials. At first these discoveries may not arouse suspicion, but as the atmosphere of the marriage changes, suspicions grow.

As these fears intensify, the apprehensive spouse sometimes asks indirect, casual questions in order to confirm these concerns (or in the hope of dismissing them). In our story, Joyce asked Robert about a discovered earring one night, and then confronted her husband the next morning. However, a person may ask such questions for quite some time before deciding upon a confrontation like Joyce's.

When a confrontation occurs, it is common for the offending spouse to lie or to even launch a counterattack.[2] Often, the faithful spouse initially accepts the denials and turns suspicions into self-doubt. Attempts are made to continue life as usual until the suspicions return. Of course, every circumstance is unique. But a repeated cycle of suspicion, confrontation, denial, and self-doubt is not uncommon.

Later, couples that enter the process of restoration encounter many obstacles that result from this cycle. When the perpetrating spouse mixes nonchalance with counterattacks, his or her spouse becomes confused and sometimes self-berating, and when the innocent spouse later realizes the level of manipulation that has occurred, a great deal of anger is often the result. This anger will be greatly intensified if the cheating spouse has used counterattacks along with denial.

For instance, even though Robert knew he was being unfaithful to Joyce, he turned the situation around and blamed her for the confrontation: "You always think the worst of me," he said. In order to deflect attention away from his own sin, he attacked his wife's integrity. In reality, these attacks may actually be stronger than the one Robert employed. Frequent responses include: "You're crazy!" and, "If you weren't so paranoid, our marriage would be better. It's your suspicious nature that is causing all of our problems!" Cursing, ranting, and raving are common at this stage, and because the innocent spouse longs to believe his or her life partner is being faithful, the innocent spouse accepts the criticism as factual, until new evidence arouses suspicions again. When the affair is finally confirmed, the innocent spouse realizes the depth of the attack that was undertaken in order to deflect attention away from the adultery, and a great deal of pain is usually the result.

Another pattern seen in counseling is denial on the part of the faithful spouse. For example, Joyce knew that Robert was lying, but still she doubted her own judgment. She didn't want to believe that the adultery was happening, and so she turned against herself and behaved in ways that actually invited self-hatred. Vacillations between certainty and uncertainty, between anger and meekness, and between acceptance and denial are common reactions during this period of suspicion and discovery.

The Sermon

"Sex," said the pastor. A silence fell over the congregation.

"Oh, pardon me," he said in mock apology. "We aren't supposed to talk about that at church, are we? But why not? Why not talk about sex? Why not preach about it from the pulpit? Is it not one of God's most beautiful gifts? Is it not one of the strongest drives within us? Why not preach about sex? God our Creator gave us this gift because He loves us. He made it enjoyable because He delights in giving good gifts to His children. Sex is intended to be a beautiful, passionate expression of romantic love.

"But don't worry. I know that we are in a room full of mixed generations. Our sermon this morning is not about the joys of sex, but the misuse of sex. Please open your Bibles and turn with me to 1 Corinthians 6:16–20."

The silence lifted and was replaced with rustling pages as the members of the congregation looked up the verses. Joyce found the passage in her Bible and followed along as it was read from the pulpit. On the pew between Robert and herself lay Robert's Bible, unopened. She noticed he seemed distracted, as though he hadn't heard a word the preacher was saying.

"Do you not know that he who is joined to a harlot is one body with her?" the pastor read. "For 'the two,' He says, 'shall become one flesh.' But he who is joined to the Lord is one spirit with Him. Flee sexual immorality. Every sin that a man does is outside the body, but he who commits sexual immorality sins against his own body. Or do you not know that your body is the temple of the Holy Spirit who is in you, whom you have from God, and you are not your own?"

"Throughout history God has coupled infidelity with idolatry."

Joyce felt Robert stiffen. *Idolatry?* she thought. *What does that have to do with infidelity?* She wondered if Robert was asking himself the same question or if she had just imagined his reaction. She tried to focus on the pastor's words.

"In the book of Jeremiah, God calls Israel 'unfaithful.' He is angered by her sin of idolatry, which is the worship of gods other than Himself. Although the Israelites belonged to the

Lord, they were giving their allegiance to an idol. They were giving that which was not theirs to give. And the someone to whom they were giving themselves had no right of ownership. In effect, Israel was saying, 'I choose to worship something that has no claim on me.' This is a violation of sacredness. Repeatedly, God calls it 'adultery.' The Israelites were guilty of it, and I dare say, there are some people sitting in this room today who are guilty of the same sin."

Robert stiffened again. This time she was certain. Although it wasn't warm in the room, beads of sweat began to form on his forehead.

"Marital adultery is a violation of sacredness every bit as much as Israel's idol worship was. First Corinthians says that our bodies do not belong to ourselves.[3] They belong to our mates. When we give ourselves sexually to someone who is not our spouse, we give away something that is not ours to give. We give it to someone who has no right to claim it.

"But what about those who are not married? Do you belong to yourself? Do you have the right to give yourself to whomever you choose? No. You have been bought with a price. You are not yours to give. You belong to God. You are His to give. And the good news is, so is your spouse—or future spouse, as the case may be. God's desire is to give good gifts to His children. That is why He warns us so often about sexual sin. It's for our protection. He loves us and wants to keep us from unnecessary harm."

Joyce thought back to her dating days with Robert. *I gave myself to him too soon,* she realized. *I never thought about myself as God's gift to Robert, or of him as God's gift to me.*

"Our passage this morning," the pastor continued, "brings to light some of God's thoughts about adultery and the protection He wants to give us. Some people say to me,

'So what if I have sex before marriage? God will forgive me. It's no worse than gossip or prideful thoughts. God says sin is sin. It's all the same. If He forgives one sin, He will forgive them all.' In the first place, this is an attitude of unrepentance and unwarranted boldness in the face of a holy God. It suggests a complete disregard for the price God chose to pay for the forgiveness He offers. But it is also based upon a false premise. Yes, it's true that in one sense all sin is sin. Each sin—regardless of the importance we humans place on it—cost Christ His life. And it is equally true that our God is a loving Father who is willing to forgive us of all of our transgressions, no matter how trivial or severe we may believe them to be. However, look back with me again to 1 Corinthians 6. We see that in this passage, God says something that He says about no other sin. God targets sexual sin as a strong offense that affects the entire person. Think about that for a minute. When you engage in a sexual act, your entire being is consumed in what you are doing. Your body, soul, and spirit are being united with another person. Verses 16 through 20 say that the act of sexual intercourse joins two people together. They become one to some degree."

Ever since Robert had started coming home late, Joyce had ridden a roller coaster of suspicion and denial. Her attempt to confront him this morning had only served to intensify her confusion. Now the pastor's sermon was introducing new issues into the whirlwind. She hadn't realized that if her suspicions were correct, Robert was not only sinning against her, but he was also sinning against himself. He was harming himself in a way she could not understand. Then she thought of Teresa. Joyce couldn't stand the thought that Robert might be joined with her—body, soul, and spirit.

How could he? How could he unite himself that way with another person?

"Breakups are excruciating experiences," said the pastor. "And when sexual relations have begun, the breakup is more difficult and causes more grief for both parties. Frequently I am called upon to counsel young people who are facing this issue. Again and again I see that when a person loses a relationship that he or she felt was going somewhere, the trauma is much greater if there has been sexual involvement. His or her body must now ignore a powerful drive whose outlet is suddenly cut off. And the soul feels like it has been ripped apart. Indeed, it may have been. During sexual intimacy, the two have become as one."

If Robert is cheating on me, thought Joyce, *will he be able to break it off with Teresa?* Her heart began to race. *Can I make him stop? Is that what I want? Or should I just leave him? Maybe I'll call in sick tomorrow and pack after Robert goes to work. But why should I be the one to leave? Maybe I'll just throw his stuff outside and call someone to come change the locks.* She was shocked at her own thoughts. *I can't believe this is happening to me. This can't be real. Maybe Robert is right. Maybe I'm just too suspicious.*

The pastor continued: "Another observation I have made about premarital sex is that it often leads to unhealthy marriages. This is because the one-flesh relationship has begun prematurely. Frequently, couples who have already begun a sexual relationship come to me for premarital counseling. For both partners, when the sexual relationship has started, the soul relationship has been forged. So they work hard to make the relationship succeed, and they deny the signals that might be telling them not to marry. Because they are already heavily invested, they plunge headlong into a marriage that should never take place.

"You see, in the New Testament, the words *adultery* and *fornication* are basically interchangeable. The original language of the New Testament was Greek. The Greek words that are translated *adultery* and *fornication* refer to a concept that basically means 'illicit sexual relationship.' The only sexual relationship given to us by God is the relationship between husband and wife. Within these boundaries, sex is intended to be a beautiful, joyful expression of love and commitment. Everything else is illicit and violates scriptural principles."

Joyce winced. She felt lousy enough without adding guilt about her past sin. But she knew she had already been forgiven for those choices. Several years ago, she had received Christ as her Savior. She had repented of her sins and had asked Christ to cleanse her. The Bible study teacher who helped her accept Christ had assured her that God had forgotten all of her past sins. She knew she had been cleansed. If only all of her life had then been magically transformed into a life of ease!

At the end of the service, the pastor extended an invitation for anyone who desired special prayer to come toward the platform and speak with one of the church counselors. Several people from the congregation went forward. Joyce noticed muffled sobbing from one man and wife who had come together. She was far too private to step out in front of a crowd of people and ask a counselor for prayer, but she held out a slim hope that Robert would be bolder. She stole a glance at him. He was fidgeting with his watch. Heaving a sigh, she closed her eyes and fought back tears as she breathed out a desperate prayer.

Please, God. Show me what to do. I don't know what to think anymore. If Robert is cheating on me, I'm not even sure I want to know. But I can't go on living like this. I need Your help.

Sex is a wonderful gift from God. He is the Master Designer, and He creates only good things. He created the sexual act with a beauty that symbolizes the union of two lives that merge into one. He created it with a spirituality that serves as an invisible "glue" that inexplicably bonds two souls. Out of its proper element, sex becomes destructive. It undermines the very relationship that God seeks to celebrate.

In the proper marital atmosphere of two humble givers seeking to please one another, the bedroom becomes a powerful arena of celebration. But it is this very power that can damage souls when sex is misused. God created sex as a delicate instrument to be used in a sensitive fashion.

Infidelity and fornication place sex outside its proper bounds. When one person, who is already bonded to their mate, then binds to another person, destruction begins. Adultery degrades both individuals as they share stolen goods and forbidden expressions of vulnerability with one another. Unspeakable damage is caused as the soul-bond between the adulterous partner and their spouse is ripped apart. Finally, separation from God and loss of communication with Him occurs, thereby cutting off the adulterous individual from the One who breathes life and joy into relationships.

What has been gained by this investment into a new relationship? A brightly packaged deception has been introduced into the lives of the adulterers. The outside appears to be a beautiful and exciting sense of satisfaction, but the box is empty. Sin satisfies temporarily, but then it asks for more. It never provides permanent fulfillment. In the case of adultery, two clandestine lovers are already invested heavily in the package.[4] When they begin to feel the emptiness of their relationship, they try harder to make it work. The unfaithful spouse knows that the marriage has been compromised by the adultery. Regardless of how empty the affair becomes, they feel internal pressure to make it work or the ruin of their marriage would have been too high a price to pay.

Sometimes people mistakenly believe that if the adulterous relationship seems like a better relationship than any they have had in the past, then it must be a valid relationship. Part of the drive to make the affair work comes because of this inaccurate concept of getting the *right* person into their lives. In other words, a person says to themselves, *I married the wrong person. This new person is the one whom I should have married. This is the right person for me.* The attempt to make the affair work becomes fueled by this false justification. The person thinks, *I am fixing a great wrong in my life. I am making it right.* This line of thinking becomes exceedingly complex, because it may actually have a hint of truth mixed in with the fallacies.

Often people do get married for the wrong reasons. They marry too young. They marry in order to get out of a bad situation with their parents. They marry because of an unwed pregnancy. Sometimes these people misquote Scripture to justify their fallacy. They say, "The Bible says, 'What God has joined together let no man put asunder.' Well, because God didn't put us together, therefore, I don't have to stay with my mate!"[5]

But God is omniscient. This means that He is all knowing. When wedding vows are taken before Him under poor circumstances, He is fully aware of those circumstances. Nowhere in Scripture do we find our heavenly Father saying, "Do not commit adultery—except in those cases where you shouldn't have gotten married in the first place." The God who knows all about the circumstances that led to our marriages is the same God who stated unequivocally, "Thou shalt not commit adultery." He left no exceptions.

God is also sovereign. This means that He is always correct in whatever He says and does. God sees all marriages, even if He did not approve of a particular union at its beginning. But once we enter into marriage, we have entered into a covenant. Proverbs 2:17 calls marriage "the covenant of God." This means that marriage is a binding contract that God has established. We are liable for all the details of this contract. So when a person has woven pain into his or her life by entering into a marriage that was not sanctioned by God, the situation cannot be remedied by entering into an adulterous relationship, which is clearly forbidden by God. Destruction will simply be added on top of pain.

At first, the damage may not be evident. Adultery often provides temporary gratification. However, the pleasure and happiness that is found with the new partner will soon prove to be a facade. Despite desperate attempts to maintain excitement, the new relationship will soon become a trap, requiring a heavy investment for the re-creation of such a fantasy. Much energy will be spent chasing a cheap imitation of the genuine bond that could have been found in one's own home all along.

The solution to the difficulties of marriage will not be found by going back in time to undo a mistake and correct it with a new partner. The answer has to do with repentance and inner change, not adultery. This should be good news for the person who knows that they were married outside of God's will.

Our omniscient, sovereign God is also a merciful Father. Psalm 103:4 declares that we are to bless the Lord "Who redeems your life from destruction, Who crowns you with lovingkindness and tender mercies." With God's help, a true contentment can be found in the midst of any circumstance, no matter how desperate. In fact, even when our circumstances seem like they will destroy us, God can crown our lives with His tenderness and love. The solution for a person who has entered into a marriage under sinful circumstances is to go to God in prayer, confess the sin of getting married outside of His will, commit to stay in the marriage, and then live according to God's principles and standards. He has never promised that life would be easy. But in His mercy, He has promised to provide all we need to find contentment, and even joy, through a right relationship with Him.

The Discovery

In the months that followed that first Sunday morning confrontation, Joyce made many discoveries that added to her suspicions. She was becoming more and more certain that Robert was indeed having an affair. Sometimes it almost seemed as if he wanted to be caught. She found several unexplained hotel charges on the credit-card statement, and her best friend told her that Robert had been seen with Teresa outside of work a number of times. People were beginning to gossip. Even so, when she asked him directly if he was having an affair, he continued to deny it.

The final proof came when she least expected it. After work one Friday, she decided to spend the weekend alone at a lake that was located about thirty minutes out of town. She needed time to think, and the lake had modest cabins that could be rented at reasonable rates. She and Robert used to go there for short weekend trips. After calling to reserve a cabin and tossing a few clothes into her backpack, she jotted a note to Robert, who wasn't home yet, as usual.

"Just needed a few days to myself," she wrote. "I'll be at the lake if you need me. Cabin 14." She started to lay the note on her pillow, thinking that Robert would probably not be home again until after midnight. She stopped short. *Why am I leaving this for him? Let him wonder where I am for a change!* She tore the note into pieces and tossed it into the garbage on her way out the door.

Joyce had purposely requested Cabin 14 because it was situated a little farther off the main drive than the other cabins. It wasn't as close to the lake as some of the other rentals, but that suited her just fine. She wanted seclusion and anonymity. She wanted to forget the world and all its troubles. She wanted quiet. And she wanted peace. This particular cabin was nestled in a little grove at the edge of the woods and would offer that. But just in case, she had stopped at the video store on the way over and rented a stack of DVDs. She might go for a row on the lake or a walk in the woods, or she might just hibernate in front of her portable DVD player all weekend. She hadn't decided. In keeping with her mood, she pulled her car along the side of the cabin, so that it wouldn't be easily seen from the road. It wasn't that she was trying to hide from anyone in particular— it was just that, for a few days, she wanted to disappear from the world altogether. There was no way she could have known how her desperate search for privacy would later serve to help confirm her greatest fears.

Around eight in the evening, Joyce wanted a snack. She decided to walk over to the camp's small gift and grocery shop for a package of cheese crackers. She also hoped to find a box of apple tarts or granola bars to go with tomorrow morning's coffee. She never made it that far.

As soon as she stepped out on the front porch, she saw it. There, parked beside Cabin 12, just two doors down from her own, was Robert's car. She froze in her steps, hoping that it was just another car that looked like his. She heard the sound of tires crunching over gravel and quickly stepped back inside the cabin, closing the door behind her. Peeking through the front window, she watched her suspicions become reality right before her eyes. The approaching car was a familiar one, and it pulled to a stop beside Robert's. Out stepped Teresa. The door of Cabin 12 opened, and there stood Robert, waiting to let her in.

Affairs are finally brought to light in many ways. At times friends call to say that they saw the spouse with another person, perhaps holding hands at a restaurant. Other times, the spouse's lover will actually call and admit to the affair.[6] Sometimes the strain of guilt will drive the unfaithful spouse to confess. Or, as in Joyce's case, sometimes a spouse witnesses a compromising situation.

But even when the evidence is overwhelming, many adulterers deny an affair when confronted.[7] This is often true even when they are caught cheating in their homes. Although the affair is obvious, they still attempt to maintain the secret fantasy they have created. When this fantasy collides with reality, they are ill prepared to cope, and so they continue to deny. Others will eventually admit to an affair, but they will usually minimize the situation and not be fully forthcoming.

Continual denials motivate some spouses to consider hiring a private detective. However, this approach can have disappointing, even destructive, results. Even when the investigation reveals conclusive proof, the denials usually continue. The expense of the detective's services and the trauma of reviewing the evidence can add to the devastation of the betrayed spouse. It is better to depend upon God's help to bring to light what has been done in secret.

Joyce sat in stunned silence. The window curtain beside her swayed, still crumpled from her tight grasp. They seemed to mock her, triumphant about the secret they had just revealed. As she gradually began to accept what she had seen, unimaginable pain enveloped her soul. She wanted to cry, but she felt as if a huge fist had reached through her chest and grabbed her lungs. She couldn't breathe. For now, the tears would have to wait. She had to get out of there!

Grabbing her backpack, she frantically began cramming in DVDs and clothes. The sound of breaking glass halted the frenzy. In her haste, she had knocked a glass of water off of a side table and shattered it. Clumsily she began to pick up the broken glass, but her thoughts spun wildly. Should she bang on their door? Should she confront them together? How she'd love to tear the hair right out of Teresa's head!

"Ow!" A small stream of blood trickled from her finger. She'd nicked herself on the glass. It wasn't a serious cut, but it was all that was needed to finally free the tears. The injustice of the moment overwhelmed her. Just a few yards away, Robert was in the embrace of another woman, and here she sat in the middle of the floor, crying and bleeding.

"How could you?" she screamed. She tried to choke back her sobs. "I have to get out of here." She was panting now. She could barely breathe. "I've got to go." She clamored toward the door, but stopped short. *What if they see me?* she thought. *I can't face Robert. Not yet. Not like this.* The sound of yelling grabbed her attention. She recognized Robert's voice and sprang to the window. He was standing on the cabin porch yelling at Teresa, who was screaming back at him over the roof of her car. She couldn't understand what they were saying, but the anger in their voices was unmistakable. Robert was shirtless. Teresa, who was barefooted, yanked open her car door and threw in her handbag. She tossed her high heels on the ground and attempted to slip her feet into them while still screaming over the top of the car. After a few almost comical attempts, her feet were finally shod. She screamed one last insult at Robert, flung herself into the car, slammed the door, and sped off in a flurry of flying gravel and dust.

Robert retreated back inside, slamming the cabin door behind him.

Joyce waited by the window for a few minutes to give Teresa time to completely exit the campground. Then, praying that Robert would not open his door at just that moment, she grabbed her backpack, made a dash for her car, and drove wildly home.

Years later, Joyce would remember to thank God for allowing her to arrive safely that night. She had screamed and cried the whole way. The trip, which usually took about thirty minutes, had been much quicker because she had driven like a lunatic. But it had been enough time for her pain to transform into anger. When she finally entered her house, she slammed the front door so hard that the walls shuddered. Entering her bedroom, she caught sight of her wedding picture sitting on the dresser. Hot pain shot through her soul. She slung her backpack across the dresser sending pictures, jewelry, and the remaining DVDs flying into the adjacent wall.

That was her last flare for the moment. She was emotionally exhausted. She looked silently at the wreckage on the floor. Then she lay back on her bed and stared absently at the ceiling. How was she ever going to face Robert again?

She had no idea when to expect him home. But since he had been left alone at the cabin, she suspected that he would be home earlier than usual. A plan began to form in her mind. She got up and began tidying the mess she had made. The glass on the wedding picture had cracked, but not shattered. She put it in a drawer and returned everything else to its rightful place.

Two hours later, Robert's car pulled into the driveway. She grabbed a book and curled up on the couch to give the appearance of having spent a quiet evening at home.

"Hi," she said, when he walked into the room.

"Hi."

"How was work?"

"The same."

"Work late again tonight?"

"Yeah."

"Is that where you've been the whole time?"

"Yeah, we're working on a big account."

"I tried to call around eight, but couldn't get any answers."

"That must have been when I stepped out for coffee."

"Couldn't get you on your cell phone, either." Joyce knew that their phone service did not work well at the lake.

"Musta left it on my desk."

"Didn't it say 'missed call' when you got back?"

"Didn't check. I had a lot on my mind with that account."

"Yeah, I know. You've really been working hard lately." Robert looked relieved at Joyce's evident sympathy.

"Did Teresa come to work today?"

He was making an effort to answer casually, but he looked startled. "She comes to work every day."

"Did she work late, too?"

"No. She left early."

"'Bout eight?"

His right eyebrow rose involuntarily. He was obviously taken off guard but managed to only sound annoyed when he answered. "I don't know when she left."

"Did she wear her pink shoes today?"

"What?"

"You know, that little sexy pair, with the high heels and the sandal straps across the back . . . That kind can be a little hard to put on sometimes . . . Especially if you're in a hurry."

Robert didn't answer. Joyce doubted whether he had noticed the color or style of Teresa's shoes. She knew she'd said enough to spark his memory of the earlier argument, but not enough to make him certain of his next step. He tried annoyance again.

"I have no idea what she wore today. I'm going to bed."

Oh, no, you're not, she thought.

"I've been thinking. It's been a long time since you and I have spent any time up at the lake."

He looked at her, apprehensive. She said nothing, letting it sink in. "And?" he asked.

"Well, at least, it's been a while since I've spent any time up there. How 'bout you? You been up to the lake anytime recently?"

"What are you talking about?"

"What about Teresa? Has she been up there anytime recently?" Her voice was getting more intense with each question.

"I have no idea."

"You don't, do you? You have no idea." She mocked his tone. "Well, I've always been partial to Cabin 14. You know the one that kind of sits back from the road."

Robert stared at her.

"But I think you like the one a few doors down. Don't you? You know, the one a little closer to the lake. Cabin 12, isn't it?"

Robert's eyes grew large.

"Oh, maybe I'm mistaken. I don't think *I've* ever been to Cabin 12 with you, Robert. Have I? Have you ever taken me to Cabin 12?"

She didn't give him time to answer. "Or is that just the one you use for your little hotties?" She was almost shouting now. "How many have there been? Huh, Robert? Do you use that one for all your women, or is that one saved just especially for Teresa?"

"I don't know what you're talking about."

"Don't know what I'm talking about? Don't know what I'm talking about? Well, you must be pretty stupid then, if you don't know what I'm talking about." She was shouting now. "OK, Mr. Don't-Know-What-You're-Talking-About. I'll tell you what I'm talking about. I'm talking about YOU and TERESA in Cabin 12 this weekend. THIS VERY NIGHT! Don't look so surprised, Mr. Hot Pants. And don't try to lie your way out of this one, either. I SAW YOU. That's right. You heard me. I WAS THERE. Right there in Cabin 14."

"What were—"

"What was I doing at the lake? Well, I'll tell you one thing—I sure wasn't doing what *you* were doing at the lake! *I* went up there for a little peace and quiet. Didn't even leave you a note. Wanted you to know what it was like having ME not show up at home for a change. Boy, was I in for a surprise. You didn't miss me." Her voice caught. "You didn't miss me one bit. Did you?" she screamed. "Because you weren't planning to come home tonight. You were on your way to Cabin 12."

Joyce threw her book across the room. It slammed loudly into the wall. Robert stood silently, just looking at her. For a moment, the only sound in the room was that of Joyce gasping for air between her sobs. Robert turned and went upstairs without a word.

"That's right. Go ahead and run away. You little coward." She had wanted to sound victorious, but the words sounded less like a lion's roar and more like the hiss of a house cat. The fervor had passed. She wanted to grab a baseball bat and start swinging, but she was too shaken and exhausted. She slumped down on the couch and gave way to her grief. She was surprised to look up and find Robert standing over her with a box of tissues. Mutely, he handed it to her and walked into the kitchen. In a moment, he returned with a glass of soda in each hand. He handed one to her, walked across the room, and then sat down in the high-backed chair that faced the couch.

"Looks like we need to talk," he said.

She didn't answer.

"You are right. I was at the cabin with Teresa."

Again, she said nothing.

"I was hoping you would never find out."

"Oh, I'm sure of that!" she said. "How long has this been going on?"

"Not long. Just a few weeks. What—uh—what exactly did you see?"

"What do you mean what did I see? What kind of a question is that? Was there something going on that you didn't want me to see?"

"Okay. Okay. That didn't come out right. I just wanted to know if you saw us fighting."

"So what if I did?"

"Well, that's what I wanted to tell you. That we aren't seeing each other anymore. I went up there to call the whole thing off."

Joyce didn't know what to say. Did he expect her to be happy?

"Do you think that makes everything all right? You broke up with your lover, so now I can just forget it, and we can go on with our lives?"

He didn't answer.

"'Cause it doesn't, Robert. It doesn't make it all right. You've been cheating on me, and IT'S NOT ALL RIGHT!"

He didn't say anything for a minute. "I'm sorry."

"Yeah. Well, I'm sorry, too. I'm sorry I ever met you. I'm sorry I ever married you. I'm sorry you even exist."

It was a long night for the two of them. They talked and argued for hours. Robert kept insisting that things were over between him and Teresa, and he continued to insinuate that Joyce should just let the whole matter rest. He apologized to Joyce and said that he never meant to hurt her. But he continued to minimize his betrayal of her and the marriage. Several times, Joyce ordered him out of the house. Finally, he did leave to stay at a hotel for the weekend. The topic of divorce had come up numerous times, but by the time Robert left, no decision had been made about the status of their marriage.

He came home after work that Monday, and they both attempted to go on with their lives as usual. But the tension between them was unbearable. Sometimes they quibbled over trivialities like adolescents. Sometimes they exploded into loud, angry arguments. Neither of them slept well. Things culminated several weeks later after a silent dinner.

"I need to know if there is any hope for this marriage," said Joyce.

Robert pushed away his empty plate, propped his elbows on the table, and rested his chin on the tips of his fingers. He stared blankly for a moment, then said, "I think there is. At least there is from my end."

"Don't make it sound like this is my fault."

"I just meant that I'm willing to work on our marriage. I know I hurt you. I wish I could take it back, but I can't. I don't know what else to do."

"Do you love me?" asked Joyce.

"Yes."

They said nothing for a few minutes.

"When do you think you are going to be able to forgive me?" Robert asked.

"I don't know."

Again they sat in silence.

"Sometimes I think it's hopeless," said Joyce. "I'm so angry. I don't know if I can ever forgive you . . . And then sometimes I think I have forgiven you, and it will be OK."

"What do you want to do?"

"I picked up a pamphlet at church. There's a Christian counseling center a few blocks from there. I'm thinking we might need to make an appointment."

Robert was not excited about going to talk to a counselor. But he could see that things were not going well in his marriage. Because he and Teresa worked at the same office, he spoke with her every day. He had not told Joyce, of course, but just the day before, he and Teresa had gone out for lunch to talk. He had told Teresa that he and Joyce were trying to patch things up. Still, he knew that if things didn't get better at home, Teresa was still an option for him. But he and Joyce had raised two children together. Their kids were both married, and their daughter was expecting their first grandchild. He loved Joyce, and he loved his kids. He was looking forward to becoming a grandfather. He didn't want to cause any more pain than he already had.

"OK," he said. "Make an appointment. I'll go."

The next week, the two of them arrived at Community Christian Counseling Center, where they met with Andy Perez, one of the staff marriage counselors.

The most common initial reaction from the betrayed spouse is anger. However, if the infidelity had not been strongly suspected, the anger may be preceded by a period of shock. Regardless of the circumstances, the emotions of the injured spouse usually swirl through a variety of reactions during the ensuing hours and days.

Both husbands and wives are deeply wounded when they are betrayed. But gender differences bring differing reactions to pain. When the wife is the one who is betrayed, she often vacillates between anger and an instinctive desire to save the marriage. Wives often suspect the affair well before it is finally admitted, and so the reaction of shock is not as strong as the anger and hurt that pierces them.

Women tend to analyze relationships, and they often turn the discovery of a husband's affair into a time of critical self-examination. So when a husband cheats, it is not uncommon for a wife to identify personal failures and to blame herself for his betrayal.

When the husband has been betrayed, his reactions differ slightly from that of a woman's. Men are less likely to pick up on the clues that might signify that an affair is occurring. So when the affair is brought to light, a husband's sense of shock and disbelief is often more pronounced. As the shock gives way to anger, he is less likely to vacillate from anger to self-blame or desperation to save the relationship. Although he may experience self-blame at a later period, his initial reaction is usually to verbalize to his wife (and to others) that she had no reason for doing what she did. It is not unusual for a betrayed husband to repeatedly yell at his wife such things as, "I treated you like royalty. We had a great relationship. You had no reason to cheat on me!" Sometimes a husband will feel a strong need to reconnect or to assert dominance and will demand sex from the unfaithful wife. This is especially true if the husband feels that his virility has been placed in jeopardy, which is a common reaction.

Spouses of either gender will often place blame on the third party. Wives do this as a way of making their husbands seem more innocent so that they can find it easier to forgive. Husbands do this as a way to reestablish their sense of manhood.

Regardless of the gender of the betraying spouse, or the circumstances of the discovery, adultery is a serious matter, and it introduces unspeakable pain into the marriage. The anger that results from this pain is intense. Few marriages can survive without outside assistance.

2

Admitting the Truth

The Breakup

During the next few weeks, Andy Perez helped Robert and Joyce cope with the trauma they were experiencing. He gave them hope that their marriage could survive the devastation that Robert's affair caused in their relationship. Frequently, he asked either Robert or Joyce to step out of the office so that he could work with one of them individually. At times they had separate appointments.[8]

One of the first things Andy did was to speak privately with Robert about the status of the affair. He got right to the point. "Have you broken off the relationship with Teresa?"

"Yes. I wish Joyce would believe me. My relationship with Teresa is over."

"Joyce doesn't believe you?"

"No. She heard me talking to Teresa on the phone a few days ago and went ballistic. She left and just came back home again last night."

"Why were you talking to Teresa?"

"She called to ask about a problem with an account at work."

"So you and Teresa work at the same place?"

"Yeah. She just needed to ask me something, and then we talked for a few minutes."

"So, you work together, and sometimes you talk on the phone."

"That's right. And that's all there is to it. I'm not sleeping with her anymore. I broke it all off with her."

"You mean, during the fight at the cabin? That's when you broke it off?"

"Well, not exactly."

"OK. Tell me exactly."

"Well, Joyce thinks I broke it off at the cabin. But that wasn't really when it happened. We did have a big fight. That's what she saw. Teresa wanted me to ask Joyce for a divorce, and I wasn't ready to do that."

"So, you weren't ready to divorce Joyce, but you didn't break up with Teresa, either?"

"Well, not that day. I had been thinking about calling it off with her. But I couldn't make up my mind. When we were apart, I would decide to end it. I was tired of trying to keep the whole thing together. I was starting to feel really guilty."

"But?"

"But when I'd get together with Teresa, I wouldn't be ready to break up."

"So, you never did."

"Well, after she left the cabin that day, I figured she had broken up with me."

"And had she?"

"Not really. She wanted to talk at work that Monday. But by then Joyce had already found out about everything, and I was ready to hang it all up."

"So, what did you say to Teresa?"

"I told her I'd decided to stay with my wife."

"How did she respond?"

"Well, she was mad, but she tried not to show it. We were on our lunch break in a restaurant right across from the office. She just got ice cold at first."

"And then?"

"Then she tried to get me to change my mind, but I told her that Joyce had found out about us, and that I was trying to work things out. So she asked if we could at least talk on the phone once in a while just to check in."

"And?"

"Well, she was really upset, and I didn't want her to make a scene."

"So, what did you tell her?"

"I told her that I'd always be her friend and that she could call anytime. I told her if she was ever in any trouble, that she knew where she could find me."

"It doesn't sound like you've broken it off with Teresa after all."

"But I haven't touched her since we started coming here."

"I believe you, Robert, but you left the door open for Teresa. She is still a part of your life. You need to end all contact with her."

"Well, Joyce insisted that I ask for a transfer at work. So I did. But my boss figured out why and decided to transfer Teresa instead. He said he'd been thinking about it anyway, because our relationship was interfering with work. She's moving next week."

"That's good. I was going to suggest that you do everything you could to separate yourself from Teresa, even if it meant considering resignation from your job. I'm glad that part of the situation has been resolved. But it isn't enough. You need to cease all communication with Teresa."

"How do I do that?"

"As soon as you can, preferably today, call Teresa. Tell her you are sorry that you ever began an affair with her. Tell her you will be having no further contact with her."

"She won't respond well to that."

"No. I'm sure she won't. You need to be prepared to stand firm in the face of her objections. Don't try to defend yourself or explain anything. Just keep saying, 'I'm sorry. It's over.' It may even be necessary to hang up on her."

Robert sighed heavily. He didn't say anything. Andy continued.

"After that, do not initiate any contact with her at all. The next time she calls, just hang up."

"But it seems wrong to be so mean to her. I told her that I would always be there for her."

"Yes, she will think it's mean. But it is wrong for you and Teresa to continue to share *any* kind of relationship. Doing that is cruel to Joyce. It is also unfair to Teresa because it keeps hope in her heart."

"Isn't there some other way? The last time I saw her, she looked terrible."

"I'm sure she did look terrible. Robert, the reason she looked terrible is because of her sin and your sin. The way for her to return to health is for you to get out of her life. If you are out of her life, she is free to begin her own process of healing and restoration."

"But she is such a sweet and caring person. I'm afraid that if I completely reject her, it will devastate her. I don't want to cause her any more pain than I already have."

"She might have been a sweet and caring person at one time. But you have helped her to use those godly qualities to engage in sin. You've helped her to ruin her character by getting involved with her. Her only chance for recovering the goodness God has created in her is for you to get out of her life."

"But how can I do that without hurting her? It doesn't seem very Christian to just start rejecting her."

"No. In a lot of ways it isn't right. I guess you could even say that it isn't Christian."

"See, I knew it. Then why are you telling me that I need to reject her and hang up on her and stuff?"

"This is what sin does. It destroys. It involves us in a lifestyle that is wrong and destructive. If you stay in this lifestyle, there will be destruction, and if you leave the lifestyle, there will be destruction. Further pain is unavoidable. The choice is yours. You entered into a covenant with your wife. You entered into sin with Teresa. Now you must choose the person to whom you will cause further destruction."

There was a long pause as Robert let this sink in. Finally he said, "I think I see what you're saying, but I'm not sure I can do it. It just doesn't feel right."

"Do you want to repair your marriage?"

"I'm here, aren't I?"

"And you want to rebuild trust with Joyce?"

"Yeah."

"Then you have to let go of the affair."

"But I keep telling you, I *have* let go of the affair. I haven't touched Teresa since we broke it off. I just feel responsible, that's all."

"You are responsible. You are responsible to your *wife*. You are responsible for building trust with Joyce and focusing on *her* feelings. Teresa's feelings are not your responsibility. Our hope is in God, not in ourselves. You have to rely on God to rebuild the trust in your marriage, but you can only do this by building a life of obedience to Him."

"And Teresa, will He rebuild her?"

"That is entirely up to Teresa. I'm not going to lie to you, Robert. Women who are rejected often have extreme reactions. She might pull all kinds of tricks to try to get you back. She may cause ugly scenes. She might threaten to hurt herself. She may even follow through with some of her threats. On the other hand, she may use her hurt as an opportunity to grow in her relationship with God. If Teresa will build a life of obedience to Him, God will restore her. There is no inoffensive way to end the relationship. But it must be done. Simply and quickly is the best way. God's command was that we marry one person and love that one person with our entire being. Once we violate that, we are in an area that is fraught with problems. Anything we do is going to have its own dilemma. A quick severing of the adulterous relationship is required. Jesus said that if your eye offends you, pluck it out. If your right hand offends you, cut it off."[9]

Robert looked shocked. "I've always been confused about that verse."

"Well, now isn't the time to get into a theological debate about literally plucking out an eye or cutting off a hand. But one message is clear: We are to completely cut ourselves off from the things that cause us to sin. In your case, your relationship with Teresa is causing you to sin. It must be cut off. You will not progress in restoring your marriage until you are completely cut off from Teresa. You don't realize it, but you are continuing your affair by staying in touch with her."

"What do you mean?"

"You are acting in the role of husband to her. Sex is not the only need a mate fulfills."

"I still don't get it."

"I'm talking about intimacy. When you are talking with Teresa and pleading for her to understand, you are relating to her on an intimate emotional level."

"It doesn't feel intimate."

"Not all intimate feelings are pleasant. Any form of vulnerability with another person is a form of intimacy. You are still giving Teresa what you should only be giving to Joyce."

Robert didn't say anything for a few minutes. "I never thought about it like that."

"I know I'm asking you to do something that is difficult. But if you want to repair your marriage, it is necessary."

Robert sighed. "Tell me again what I need to do."

Quite often, the perpetrator has difficulty completely breaking off contact with the adulterous partner. Sometimes it becomes almost a compulsion for the perpetrator to want to say good-bye more than once. There is a strong desire to check with the adulterous partner's feelings and make sure they are okay with the good-bye. Although it may be cloaked in a veil of compassion, this concern is an unhealthy drive. It keeps the affair alive and works against the restoration of the marriage. This tendency needs to stop. There is no allowance for "give and take" on this issue.

If there is to be any hope of restoring the marriage relationship, the unfaithful spouse must break off all contact with the adulterous partner. This may seem like an obvious statement. Yet many people continue some form of contact even while claiming that the sexual relationship has come to an end. Because a one-flesh relationship has been established, the two parties are bonded. Therefore, the only way to restore the marriage is to completely sever that bond.

This should be done in one conversation, preferably by telephone. There are two components that need to be included: an admission of guilt, and a declaration of finality. For instance, a man such as Robert should say, "I never should have gotten involved with you. I was wrong, and I am sorry. I have sinned against you, against my wife, and against God. I am going to work things out with my wife. I know that this hurts you, but it's over. I will not be contacting you anymore. Please do not try to contact me." This should be done once, and only once.

After these words are said, the conversation needs to end. Often the other person will not accept the breakup gracefully. They usually respond with contradiction, enticement, and pleading. Instead of arguing, these reactions from the other person need to be met with the simple response, "I'm sorry. It's over." If the other person asks questions such as "Why?" the response should be, "I'm sorry. It's just over." If the person requests a final meeting or desires to continue innocent conversations, "just to see how you are doing," the response needs to be "No. I'm sorry. It's over." No attempt should be made to explain or defend the decision. The call should be kept short, even if this necessitates abruptly hanging up. If the lovers continue talking, then guilt, lust, or feelings of loss may cause them to meet again. The caller needs to be prepared to stand firm.

People enter into counseling with therapists and pastors with varying circumstances and in varying stages of a breakup. Keeping the following principles in mind will help:

1. The wronged spouse needs to insist that the affair end immediately. They may be tempted to give instructions about

what the offending party should say when breaking up with the adulterous partner. This is not helpful. They simply need to stand firm on the two requirements of the cheating spouse: (a) end it now, and (b) inform the other person that it is indeed over. This is an immediate concern, and there is no room for negotiation.

Sometimes the injured party asks whether or not they should be present during the breakup. This is a matter of choice, depending on the people involved. The decision to do this has its pros and cons. On the positive side, some find that witnessing the breakup helps to bring a sense of security that the severing of the adulterous relationship has, in fact, occurred. It reduces suspicions and helps the couple to focus on other issues in the restoration process.

On the other hand, hearing the spouse talk to the former lover can be a painful experience. Also, the perpetrator needs to break up voluntarily and without artificial help. Willingness to face the breakup alone may actually bring more security to the relationship than having it occur with the mate present.

The adulterer needs to experience the process of ending the relationship with the other person. This is a vital part of the restoration process because it closes the door on the adulterous relationship. It causes the cheating spouse to enter into the acceptance of closure, and it brings assurance to the faithful spouse that the relationship can now begin the process of rebuilding.

2. The breakup should occur once and only once. The door needs to be firmly shut. Prolonging the breakup actually prolongs the adulterous relationship.

This is not an easy assignment. The first step is to go to God in repentance and give the relationship over to Him. A sample prayer would be, *Heavenly Father, I acknowledge that this relationship is sin. It is wrong. It is not from You. I choose to have nothing to do with it. I ask for the ability to end it in grace and in righteousness.*

3. The ending should be brought about in a manner that is as detached and objective as possible. A face-to-face confrontation is not recommended, primarily because it involves seeing the adulterous partner again. This gives them seductive power and sets up the opportunity for unnecessary temptation. It also makes it difficult to cut off the conversation and leave.

Some counselors suggest writing a letter. While a letter is certainly better than a face-to-face meeting, we do not recommend it. Anytime a person puts something like this in writing, it gives the other person ammunition for argument and retaliation. The telephone is a good medium for a breakup because it is removed from the other person, yet allows for some verbal communication.

4. The cheating spouse needs to be prepared for the reaction of the other person. There has been a heavy investment into the adulterous relationship, and the third party rarely lets go easily. Therefore, any effort to engage in argument, explanation, or pacification plays right into the needs and desires of the other person. Even unpleasant contact is a continuation of the relationship. Attempts at further contact by the lover are not to be indulged and should be met by hanging up the telephone, by closing the door, or by walking away. This provides the wounded spouse the opportunity to witness their mate's determination to stand firmly committed to their relationship and aids the reestablishment of trust in the marriage.

5. The faithful spouse needs to be informed of what took place during the breakup conversation. They need to know how the breakup took place and what might be expected as a result of the breakup. For example, a husband might say, "It is likely from what she said, that she might call and want to talk to me. I want you to know that I am making a commitment to you and to God.

She might try to chase me, but I want nothing to do with her. If she calls our house, go ahead and hang up on her. If I answer, I'll hang up on her. If I see her somewhere, I'll turn around and walk the other way. If she shows up at our house, I will close the door and not go outside. The relationship is officially over, and I am totally committed to focusing on you and me 100 percent from now on." The adulterer, as a part of restoration and rebuilding, needs to go through the process of saying these things.

6. It is important to note that the reactions of both the other person and the injured spouse might not be satisfying to the repentant spouse. The other person will be hurt. The breakup will cause a wounding, but this wounding is a result of sin. Both adulterers need to realize the damage that sin does. Trying to protect the lover from this pain only prolongs and intensifies the damage done to the marriage, to the former lover, and to the perpetrator's relationship with God.

In addition to dealing with the negative reaction from the former lover, the repentant spouse may also receive a negative reaction from their mate. When a husband or wife says, "I have broken it off with the other person. I am now completely committed to you," a spouse may feel insulted. Such a statement could be equivalent to hearing someone say, "I borrowed your car without your permission. It has a smashed hood and three flat tires, but don't worry, you can have it back now." If a spouse feels that they are receiving "used goods" from the straying partner, it is perfectly acceptable to express this feeling. This is a legitimate reaction. The inability of the faithful spouse to gracefully accept these initial statements is a consequence of the pain caused by the adultery, and the adulterer needs to accept this. The faithful spouse needs the healing effect of hearing statements of recommitment, despite the doubts that may arise. If the straying spouse is consistent with this commitment over a long period of time, a foundation can be laid for a vibrant and restored marriage.

7. Finally, it is important for counselors and pastors to note that some issues are better discussed privately with the perpetrator. This is especially true when dealing with the issues of breaking off the relationship with the third party and with the adulterer's tendency to grieve at the loss of the affair. Sometimes the perpetrator wants to express this grief to the counselor in a joint session, when both the husband and wife are present. These feelings are real and need to be discussed. But the expression of these feelings in the presence of the victim would cause unnecessary pain. The counseling process does not need to cause this kind of further wounding, and doing so could create scars that will not heal. The counselor needs to meet with the offending spouse individually so that these issues can be fully discussed and resolved.

A Full Confession

The week after Robert's phone call to Teresa, he and Joyce came to their session obviously angry.

"I don't know what she wants from me," said Robert. "Nothing I do is right. I thought she would be happy that I called Teresa and broke up with her. But when I came home and told her about it, she blew up."

"Of course, I blew up. You had told me it was already over. You said you broke it off with her that night at the cabin."

"Well, it was already over, kind of."

"What do you mean, 'kind of'? How can it be 'kind of' over? Either it's over or it's not. Besides, you told me that this whole thing was no big deal. Why did she need some big official send-off anyway?"

"Huh?" He was caught off guard.

"You said that you'd been with her a few weeks. Is she so dumb that she couldn't figure out that it was over after your fight at the cabin?"

Robert didn't know what to say. He knew that Andy was aware of the length of the affair. He didn't want to lie in front of Andy, but he knew if Joyce learned the affair had been serious, she might never forgive him. So, he said nothing.

Andy could see that something was wrong. "Joyce, would you mind giving Robert and me a few minutes alone?"

After Joyce left, Andy said, "Have you allowed Joyce to believe that your relationship with Teresa was only a few weeks?"

"Yes."

"Why?"

"Well, the night she found out, I was trying to calm her down. I told her that Teresa and I had broken up and that the affair hadn't lasted very long."

"Robert it is important that you be completely honest with Joyce about everything you say if you want to restore trust in the marriage."

"I know that. I really haven't been trying to lie to her anymore, but I thought that if I went back and told her those things, that it would just make matters worse."

"Worse for whom?"

Robert looked at Andy without speaking. Finally he said, "Worse for both of us, really. Joyce is already hurt and angry, won't learning more about the affair make it harder?"

"Yes. It will make it harder. It will make her angry. It will cause more hurt. But it will not cause near the difficulty that your continued lying will cause."

There was silence.

"She might not ever be able to forgive me."

"She will know if you continue to lie. And you are right, when she learns the truth, she may not choose to forgive you. That is the risk you take. But if you continue to lie, you guarantee that the relationship will never be restored. A restored relationship requires humility and honesty. If you want to rebuild trust with Joyce, a full confession is necessary. No more minimizing the situation. No more pretending it was no big deal. Even if you had only slept with Teresa once, it would have been a big deal. It would have been a major betrayal. But you had a yearlong, full-blown affair. If you try to pretend that it was a short-term fling, the evidence will stack up against you. Joyce will know you are lying, and she will not believe you are capable of becoming a trustworthy husband."

After talking with Andy awhile, Robert understood that he needed to make a full confession to Joyce. Andy invited Joyce back into the session and asked her if she would be willing to make a follow-up appointment for the next day. He knew that she was going to need further support.

That afternoon, Robert was finally honest with Joyce about the full scope of the affair. He admitted that he had been involved with Teresa for about a year. He admitted that the fight at the cabin had not been the result of his breaking up with her, but a result of his unwillingness to leave Joyce and marry Teresa, as Teresa desired. He confessed that he had continued to speak with Teresa on his lunch breaks until recently and told her in detail what had occurred when he called Teresa and broke up with her. Andy had advised him to answer all of Joyce's questions honestly, and he did.

Of course, Joyce was angry to learn much of what she was hearing. But she was not surprised. In fact, it was Robert who was surprised to learn that having all of the facts was a form of relief for Joyce.

"I thought this had been going on for a while," she said at one point. "Things were adding up. I felt like I was going crazy."

It was a long, tearful conversation. But it was an important step down the path of restoration.

∾

Rebuilding trust is a nonnegotiable aspect of restoring a marriage after infidelity. Without trust, there can be no healthy, life-giving intimacy. And without honesty, there can be no trust.

When a cheating spouse finally admits the affair, the tendency is to minimize its scope and depth in order to avoid further discomfort. But eventually the wronged spouse will begin to suspect that everything is not as it seems, and the gap of mistrust widens. It is important, therefore, that the wandering spouse give a full account of their actions.

This is done in two ways. First, it is important that the questions asked by the faithful spouse be answered honestly and completely.[10] Second, making a full confession of the affair to the spouse is a vital step. The lies and minimization need to end. Truth needs to take its rightful place in the marriage. Several items should be included in this confession:

1. An admission of the duration of the affair;
2. An accounting of when, how, and where the affair started;
3. A confession of any lies that have been told during or after the affair, and a replacement of these lies with the truth;
4. An admission of any contact that has been made with the other person after the affair was discovered; and

5. An honest answer to any question that is asked by the faithful spouse.[11]

Should All Affairs Be Confessed?

Occasionally a person will come to a pastor or counselor with a burden of guilt about an affair that occurred many years ago. The question is raised, "Should I confess my indiscretion to my mate?"

Opinions vary on this issue. Sometimes well-meaning people advise the offender to confess, due to a belief that secrets hurt the marriage. However, we do not recommend the confession of affairs that ended many years ago. Admissions like these have caused much damage to relationships. Usually, the motive for the confession is to find relief from overwhelming guilt that comes from the affair, and the offending spouse experiences great relief after confessing the sin. But this relief comes at a cost. The wounded spouse often has difficulty in overcoming the information, and an unnecessary rift occurs in the marriage.

Our suggestion is that if the affair has been over for several years, if all contact with the other person has been terminated, and if the guilty party has been restored to a vibrant relationship with God, then the burden needs to be carried by the offender alone. The burden is a natural consequence of the sin that occurred. It can be relieved through confession and repentance before God, discipleship, and a growing relationship with God. However, there is no need to burden the mate with the painful discovery of the affair.

3

Dissolving the Lies

The Lie of Grief

One afternoon, in a private session between Andy and Robert, Andy asked for permission to allow a counseling intern to participate in the session. Robert agreed, and Suzannah Freeman was allowed to join them in their time together.

"I'm hurting so much," said Robert, "I don't know what to do. Sometimes I wonder if it's worth all of the effort to work it out with Joyce."

"Tell me more about what you mean."

"Well, I can see that I have really hurt Joyce. I'm not sure she will ever forgive me, and I don't blame her, and—well, the damage is already done."

"So . . ."

"So why don't I go on and be with the woman I love?"

"Who is . . . ?"

"Teresa."

"So you're saying that you are in love with Teresa, and you don't want to resolve things with Joyce."

"No, not exactly. It's just that it doesn't seem worth it sometimes. I know the affair was wrong. I know that fixing it up with Joyce is the right thing to do. But I can't help it. I miss Teresa."

"Tell me more about what you are feeling."

"Teresa was good for me. We were great together. She made me feel strong. It was like a Hollywood romance or something. She thought I was terrific, and I thought she was incredible."

"So, when you were with Teresa, you felt good."

"Yes. She listened to me. She encouraged me. She made me feel important. She was always building me up. You know, telling me how good I am at my job, or at fixing her car, or whatever . . . I miss her so much."

Suzannah said, "It sounds to me as if you are grieving over your lost relationship with Teresa."

"Grieving?"

"Yes, you had a relationship with Teresa. It was wrong, but it was real. Now that it's over, you miss it. You know it would be wrong to go back to it, but you still miss what that relationship gave you."

"Yes, that's it! That's exactly how I feel. I want to do the right thing, but I can't get Teresa out of my mind."

"Well," said Suzannah, "any time you end a relationship, a period of grief is normal."

"Yes, that's true," said Andy. "But in your case, Robert, I don't recommend that you allow yourself the right to grieve."

Both Robert and Suzannah looked at him in surprise.

"Robert, you had feelings and emotions while you were having the affair with Teresa, but those feelings were based on a lie."

"She never lied to me!"

"I don't mean her lies—I mean yours."

"What do you mean?"

"You believed that her encouragement, praise, and compliments were the same thing as love. As long as you were having your self-esteem built up by Teresa, you felt you needed to be with her."

"That's exactly how I felt."

"But the feeling was built on a lie. You didn't need Teresa to build up your self-esteem. There are many other ways to have one's self-esteem built up without getting involved in an affair."

"But I fell in love with Teresa!"

"I've no doubt that you felt strong emotions while you were involved with Teresa, but you don't need to confuse those feelings with love."

"It sure felt like love."

"Love is based on truth. The truth is, your soul was bonded to Joyce's at the time of the affair. Your relationship with Teresa was not an act of love, but an act of betrayal. Teresa made you feel built up, but in reality, you were degrading yourself—and Joyce. When you were with Teresa, you felt like a strong person, but you were actually giving in to your weakness. You believed a lie. The emotions you felt were not based on truth. They were based on lies."

"But Teresa is a good person."

"This isn't about Teresa. It's about you. You believed that being with Teresa was a good thing. It wasn't. It was destructive."

"But I do have some good memories of our times together."

"Yes, but those memories are also based on lies. You were living a fantasy together. You said it yourself. It was like some Hollywood romance . . . something orchestrated to entertain and please. Your relationship was not based on love; it was based on self-indulgence. You had enjoyable feelings when you were with her, and you mistook those feelings for love."

"If it wasn't love, then what was it?"

"It was a fantasy, a wild ride, a fun time. But it was not love. Love involves commitment, self-sacrifice, and faithfulness. An act of unfaithfulness cannot at the same time be an act of love. The two are mutually exclusive."

"So, I am just supposed to grieve quietly."

"No, not even that."

Robert was stunned. Andy was usually more sympathetic.

"I know this is painful for you to hear, but you have to learn to live in truth. What I have discovered after counseling many couples like you and Joyce is that grieving over the loss of an adulterous relationship hinders growth."

"You mean the growth of my relationship with Joyce."

"Yes, and I mean your personal growth, as well."

"I don't get it."

"Robert, adultery is sin. Scripture admonishes us to abandon sin . . . to hate it. Grieving over lost sin will keep the effects of that sin alive in your soul."

"But I have repented already. Didn't my sin get taken away?"

"Yes, that's true. The moment you repented, God cleansed you and reconciled His relationship with you. But sin causes damage. It affects you. Repentance didn't automatically erase all of its effects. One of the effects is that you feel pain at the loss of your relationship with Teresa. If this had been a relationship based upon truth and goodness, allowing yourself the process of grief would help to heal you. But the relationship was based upon falsehood and sin. If you grieve over lost sin, you keep the longing for that sin alive in your soul."

"Well, how do I get rid of it, then? I'm miserable."

"One way of dealing with your loss is to recognize the affair as sin. Recognize it as something that had to be lost. When you begin to feel the pain of the loss of Teresa in your life, verbalize these thoughts."

"Verbalize? You mean, say, 'That was wrong. Too bad, so sad!'?"

"No, not, 'Too bad, so sad.' Let's say you are feeling pain over the fact that you are missing Teresa. You miss talking to her and having her listen to you and encourage you. Or you may even miss having sex with her. What you need to do is go to God in prayer and say something like this: 'Heavenly Father, I have lost nothing that is necessary for my life. What I lost was sin. And that sin was destructive to me. Therefore, I declare to You that I am glad it is over. It is good for me that it is over. I have made the right choice. I am staying with You.'"

Robert left the session in a somber mood. He knew he had a lot to think about in the days ahead. After he left, Andy and Suzannah met to talk.

"I was surprised at your reaction to Robert today," Suzannah began.

"You were expecting me to do grief therapy?"

"Well, yes. He seems to be grieving over the loss of his relationship with Teresa."

"True, but he has no right to that grief."

"Well, I agree that he had no right to the affair, but grief is a natural part of the human process. It is neither good nor bad. Aren't we supposed to do what is best for the client? We aren't supposed to superimpose our own moral judgments on him."

"I understand your concern. As a matter of fact, it is one of the reasons I asked you to observe this particular session as a part of your internship. Based on a few comments Robert has made in recent sessions, I felt sure this issue was going to surface soon. You asked about doing what is best for the client. I believe that grieving the loss of his relationship with Teresa is truly bad for him."

"I don't understand. If he doesn't allow himself to grieve, won't he be repressing his feelings? I mean, whether we think he has a right to them or not, his feelings are still very real to him. He has to respond to them in some way."

"That's true. His feelings are real. But he needs to deal with them based on truth. The truth is, adultery is bad for people. It was bad for him and bad for Joyce and bad for Teresa. Adultery is based upon deceit and self-indulgence. That is not a foundation for a healthy relationship."

"You have no argument from me on that point. But isn't that history? The deed has been done."

"In a way, that's exactly my point. The deed has been done, and it needs to stay in the past. Robert does not need to keep bringing it to the forefront of his memory. Part of grief is longing for something. If he allows himself the freedom to grieve, he is opening himself to the incredible pain of longing for his sin to return. He will long to do things that are destructive to him. That's no good. He will either be stuck with a longing that will stay unfulfilled and harm him, or he will give in to the longing and cause further damage."

"But won't the grief process help him get over his longing?"

"Healthy grieving helps reduce longing, not alleviate it. When a person loses a loved one and grieves, the longing to be with the one they have lost does not go away, but it does become manageable. The goal of grieving is not to rid oneself of longing. It is to adjust to the loss. However, the goal of Robert's healing is to help him be rid of his longing for Teresa altogether. I have found that this is rarely accomplished by grieving."

"How is it accomplished?"

"By living in the truth. By speaking the truth to God. By using the feelings of longing for Teresa as a trigger to speak the truth about the affair to himself and to God."

"Hmm. I've never heard this before."

"Well, to tell you the truth, neither have I. It is something I have come to believe after years of working with couples like Robert and Joyce. Over and over again, I have seen that when a client grieves over a legitimate loss, the grieving allows him to let go. It eventually eases the pain. Conversely, those who grieve over the loss of something sinful tend to hang on instead of letting go."

"That's interesting. I guess it does make sense. It seems you are saying that grieving over sin actually causes the person to focus on the sin. The process of grieving actually becomes a sort of stumbling block, setting up a temptation to return to the sin."

"Exactly."

"But even though Robert has sinned, aren't his feelings legitimate? How can we teach someone to be forthright and honest with his feelings if we are going to turn around and negate some of those very same feelings?"

"That is a legitimate concern, and it requires much thoughtfulness and prayer on the part of the counselor. The perpetrator needs to tell his story. He needs to dig into his memory and soul and tell all that is going on in his life. He needs to talk to his counselor about when he got involved in the affair. He needs to tell how it developed . . . the whole story. He also needs to talk about how he felt then, to share the dreams he had about the relationship. And he needs to talk about how he now feels about the affair. He needs to get all of it out, and it is guaranteed not to come out in a neat package. He will mix legitimate issues with issues that were based upon his sin."

"It seems as if you're contradicting yourself."

"Well, it's at this point that the role of the counselor is critical. The counselor must help the client discern truth from the lie. He needs to help the client learn to tell the difference between proper grieving and holding on to sin."

"How do we do that?"

"Well, first with much prayer and dependence on the Holy Spirit."

"OK."

"But the primary role is to tell the truth."

"What do you mean?"

"Well, a person might say, 'I really miss my mistress. She met all of my needs. I have never found anyone like her before.' That is a lie. It is truly how the client feels, but his feelings are based upon false beliefs. Sin cannot meet our needs."

"So what would you say to the client in that situation?"

"I would say just that. 'You are believing in a lie. She did not meet your needs, because sin cannot meet your needs. You liked the way it felt, but it was taking you deeper into sin. Ultimately it has cost you dearly.'"

"I see. So you don't deny the person's feelings. You try to show him the lie that fuels those feelings."

"Yes, and more than that. The goal is to help the client replace the lie with the truth. In this case, to help him understand how damaging and dangerous the game was that they were playing, regardless of how good it felt."

"I sat in on a session earlier today where the client said to the counselor, 'If my wife and I had an adequate sexual relationship, and if we had been communicating like we used to, I would not have gotten into this affair.' That statement had some truth to it. How would you respond to that?"

"Well, many times clients will say things that have the truth and a lie mixed together. The man was making a valid point. The missing ingredients in his marriage did contribute to his becoming vulnerable. But the sin belongs to him and him alone. The book of James tells us that sin must not be softened or excused by circumstances. Adultery is evil. It did not come from God."[12]

"So you are saying that the client needs to express everything to his counselor. But the counselor may have to help him discern the truth from the lies."

"Exactly. If he doesn't tell his story, it will stay within him and become an obstacle to healing. However, the lie must not have repeated expression or it will grow. Expressing truth lightens burdens and weakens the negative effects of events. Expressing a lie strengthens negative memories. Expressing the lie repeatedly can keep a person enslaved to the negative effects."

"I see. So that is why you said earlier that grieving the sin is bad for Robert."

"Right. Grieving involves repeated expression of feelings. In the case of adultery, the feelings are based upon a sinful reality. And any repeated expression of them will make them stronger."

The next day Joyce came in for her private session with Andy. "I don't know what to do. Robert can't get over Teresa. I don't know how to help him."

"Tell me what you mean."

"Well, he mopes around the house looking sad. I ask him what's wrong, and sometimes he won't answer. Other times he only says that it's hard to adjust to life without Teresa in it. He keeps telling me not to take it personally, and that he loves me. But he still feels the loss of her in his life. It really hurts me to hear him say that. I hate hearing him talk about his feelings for Teresa. But he seems to be trying to work on the marriage, so I try to listen."

"And when he talks about it, how do you feel?"

"I want to explode! I feel so angry! But I know I should try to help him through it. So I keep it all inside and let him talk. After all, I want him to get beyond this. But it seems like it's taking forever. He's been talking about it off and on for weeks."

"Joyce, I admire your willingness to help Robert in his pain, but this is one time you don't have to be sympathetic."

"I don't?"

"No. And I have recently begun working with Robert on this issue. It is not good for him to give in to his feelings of grief over the affair. He needs to see the affair as his enemy. When he grieves the affair, he is grieving for sin. This is not good for him."

"What should I do?"

"Be yourself. Don't feed the grieving. If you want to, you can confront it. When he starts talking about Teresa, tell him how that makes you feel. But, if you don't feel like discussing it, that's OK, too. Just tell Robert you don't want to hear about his feelings toward Teresa. You don't have to fix it. And you don't have to go through the pain of listening to his feelings. Robert and I are dealing with this in our private sessions. So don't feel like you have to carry his burden. Your rejection of his grief will help him to see it for what it is. Let's not give him any reason to hang on to it."

~

After a person has experienced the loss of a significant relationship, they experience feelings of grief. Something that was important is no longer present. A relationship that the person believed was a source of many benefits has dissolved. This is painful. The natural response is one of grief. However, it is important to examine the difference between legitimate grief and illegitimate grief.

Legitimate grief results from a relationship that is based upon truth. Human beings need relationships. We are created as interdependent beings. We need a healthy amount of dependence on other people in order to survive and to experience nurture. When we lose the presence of a significant person in our lives, we need to allow ourselves the freedom to grieve that loss. The rejection of a close friend, the death of a spouse, or the relocation of a family member are all examples of losses that result in legitimate grief. This kind of grief needs attention, time, and tears. Eventually, the pain eases, and the power of grief will lessen.

Time spent grieving over sin has the opposite effect. Illegitimate grief results from a relationship that is based upon falsehood. There is no doubt that the loss of an adulterous relationship is a significant and painful loss, but it is the loss of a sinful relationship. The pleasurable feelings experienced during the relationship were real and enjoyable. But they were based upon falsehood. The two persons involved believed that they needed and loved one another. Yet, they were simply using one another to meet their own self-centered desires. Perhaps they felt needed, important, excited, or courageous. But in reality, they were setting themselves and one another up for destruction. Relationships based upon falsehood and sin can never meet a person's ultimate needs. Pain

~

is the inevitable result. Time and attention spent grieving a relationship of this type does not result in healing. Instead, it awakens the longing for the sin's return. It must be rejected, or it will grow and lead once again in the wrong direction.

Thus a question is raised: If the feelings are real, but based upon false beliefs, how are they to be handled? Should they simply be disregarded and ignored? No, they do not need to be ignored, but they must be overcome. This is only accomplished by living in truth. A habit of speaking the truth to God can be developed. When feelings of longing for the adulterous partner arise, they can be used as triggers to speak the truth about the affair to God and to oneself.

The key to working through this difficult task is to focus upon the truth. This helps a person learn how to be vulnerable and open while ridding themselves of false beliefs that will cause a return to sin. On the other hand, the task does not involve just weeding out the false beliefs. A pastor or counselor can also help discover the truth about the perpetrator's inner character and emotional framework. For instance, if the offender says, "She (he) made me feel needed," a truth about their soul has been revealed, but a false belief has also been exposed. The counselor can affirm that everyone needs to feel needed, but he should also point out the false belief about needs.[13] The perpetrator should come to realize that their former lover didn't actually *need* the adulterous relationship. The lover may have *wanted* the relationship, but he or she did not need it. Neither did the perpetrator need the lover. By entering into an affair, destruction was invited into both of their lives. No one needs to experience the kind of devastation that infidelity brings!

But there is a glimmer of truth that can be used to help in discipleship and to encourage continued vulnerability. There was a *desire to feel needed*. This can be followed up. Why was the issue of being needed so important? Why did this arouse temptation? The issue of wanting to be needed can be discussed, and the perpetrator can be helped in their spiritual growth through the discussion. It is possible to fulfill this perfectly acceptable desire in a healthy, biblical manner.

In other words, the desire to grieve over the loss of an affair does not result in spiritual health if a person gives in to it. However, if the person is brave enough to discuss these feelings with a caring counselor, the feelings can gently be used as tools to aid in changing the inner being. They are fertile ground in which the Holy Spirit can work to forge the betrayer's character to become more like Christ.

There is a simple mechanism that can aid in this process. It centers on these four words: *decide, declare, remind,* and *refocus.*

1. **Decide:** A person needs to decide in advance that God's plan for their life is best and that all other plans lead to disaster. It is important to go to God with this decision and confess it before Him. For example, a husband might pray something like this: *Father, I accept Your plan for my life. You have stated in Your Word that one woman, my wife, is all I need to satisfy my desires for companionship and sexual fulfillment. I accept this truth. I decide today to actively pursue it.*

2. **Declare:** When feelings of loss and grief surface, they provide the opportunity for spiritual growth. These feelings can be seen as an opportunity to remind the individual of the decision to live in God's truth. This is done through a simple prayer of declaration. For example, Robert would pray, *Father, I miss Teresa because I felt good with her. I believed I was bringing joy into my life, but in reality I was bringing pain to myself and to my wife. You have given me everything I need in my wife. If I invest in her, she*

brings encouragement to me. Even if she does not, I can find everything I need in my relationship with You. I declare my desire to obey You and to serve You.

Note that the primary focus of the prayer is not on the feeling, the sin, or the lie, although they are all honestly acknowledged; the primary focus of the prayer is upon the truth, which can be found in the Word of God.

3. **Remind:** Our feelings are gifts from God, designed to accomplish His good work in our lives. They are intended for our good. But once we have given Satan a foothold in our lives by entering into habitual, long-term sin, our feelings become easily distorted. It is only as we repent and receive forgiveness from God that emotional restoration can truly begin. The process of decision and declaration does not necessarily result in immediate results. This struggle is addressed, in part, through praying simple prayers, which serve as a reminder of the truth God is working in the person's life. For example, a repentant wife might pray a short prayer such as, *Heavenly Father, You have given me all I need in my husband. I will invest in him.* This kind of declaration can be of great benefit in helping to keep alive the decision to live a godly life.

4. **Refocus:** Once the decision to walk in truth is remembered and declared, then the person's thoughts need to be shifted to something completely unrelated to the affair. Some suggestions include jogging, listening to Christian music, reading a godly (but unrelated) book, memorizing favorite passages of Scripture, singing praise-and-worship music, praying for others, or going for a walk. Any innocent activity that distracts from the emotional struggle is acceptable and encouraged.

Finally, there is no reason for the betrayed spouse to be subjugated to the perpetrator's grief. Although patience and communication are desirable qualities in any marriage, it is not the role of a betrayed spouse to help the offender heal from the loss of the adulterous lover. The injured spouse is to focus on healing from the betrayal. Therefore, it is acceptable to reject the perpetrator's expression of grief over the affair.

~

The Lie of Dissatisfaction

Some weeks later, Robert and Joyce began a counseling session that would prove to be a turning point in their attempt to restore their marriage.

"I've been thinking a lot about what you said about replacing the lie with the truth," said Robert. Joyce looked at him curiously, but said nothing. Robert continued, "You told me to start declaring truth to God in prayer. Well, that's been really hard to do. But I've been trying. And some cool things have been happening. It's like God is showing me more and more truth."

"That's really encouraging," said Andy. "Tell us some of what God has been showing you."

"Well, do you have a Bible here?" Andy always kept his Bible close by during counseling sessions. He turned to a side table, picked it up, and handed it to Robert.

"Joyce and I have been going to a Bible study class at our church. Last week the lesson was from the book of Galatians. When the teacher read these verses, I couldn't believe it. It was like God whispering in my ear, *Listen up, Robert. These verses are for you.* I don't mean that I heard voices or anything, but the passage definitely got my attention."

Robert opened the Bible to Galatians 6:6–9 and began reading, " 'Let him who is taught the word share in all good things with him who teaches. Do not be deceived, God is not mocked; for whatever a man sows, that he will also reap. For he who sows to his flesh will of the flesh reap corruption, but he who sows to the Spirit will of the Spirit reap everlasting life. And let us not grow weary while doing good, for in due season we shall reap if we do not lose heart.'

"When he read that, I realized that I had been trying to mock God. I wanted to do my own thing but not face any consequences for my behavior. I wanted to have Teresa and to have Joyce, too. It was like I didn't think that God saw what I was doing. Or if He did, that He didn't care. I also realized that He loves Joyce too much to let me get away with that. And I realized something else. Something I had never thought of before. He loved *me* too much to let me get away with that. He wants me to experience a love relationship with Him, and I can't do that and live a lie at the same time."

Andy smiled. He could see that God was doing a work in Robert that no counseling session could ever accomplish. Joyce, on the other hand, looked stunned. Andy turned to her. "What do you think about what Robert's saying?" he asked.

"I'm not sure what to think," she replied. "It's good, I guess."

"Wait," said Robert. "I'm not through."

"OK, let's hear it," said Andy.

"God seems to really be showing me things right now. Even when Joyce and I argue, it's like God is saying, *Listen to her. Listen to her.* Joyce is so angry. She is bitter. I want to find fault with that. I want to say, 'She should be a better Christian. She should be more forgiving.' But it's like God is whispering to me again, *Listen to her.* That's when I began to realize, *I* did this to her. I have made her bitter. I have wounded her spirit. And it started way before the affair. I started believing lies way before I ever started going out with Teresa."

Tears began streaming down Joyce's face. Robert choked up, and for a moment, nothing was said. "Last week in Bible study, one of the guys was talking about a tough time in his marriage. He was saying how most marriages experience periods that are exciting and periods that are mundane. This is a normal part of life. He said that our culture lies to us and tells us that relationships are only about romance. If the excitement fades, the love no longer exists. I suddenly realized that I had believed that lie. I had thought my feelings were supposed to indicate the success of the marriage. I wasn't feeling fulfilled in my marriage. So I blamed it on Joyce. I failed to examine myself to see if I was contributing to the problem. She seemed angry and stressed out much of the time. It didn't occur to me that I might be the reason.

"Things were going so well at work. I felt successful there. I felt respected. But home, I felt resented. I concluded that I married the wrong person."

"Are you saying that this is all my fault?" asked Joyce.

"No!" said Robert. "Exactly the opposite. I realized how unfair I've been to you for a very long time. I'm so sorry. I have wanted you to understand my faults, to be accepting and loving, but I wasn't giving you that same grace. Every fault you have, I amplified. I was irritable and cranky and critical. I did everything I could to place the blame for my sense of dissatisfaction on you. It wasn't fair. I'm so sorry. Please forgive me."

There was another moment of silence in the room. Joyce didn't reply, partially because she was silently weeping and couldn't speak. Finally, Andy asked, "Joyce, what do you think about all of this?"

"I don't know what to think. Part of me wants to believe Robert. I've never heard him talk this way before."

"What about the other part of you?" asked Andy.

"That part of me wants to scream and throw things. I've known how unfair he has been for a long time. I've tried to tell him. I've tried to get him to listen to me. Why did it take so long for him to finally see it? Why did it take an affair to make him see?"

The three of them continued to talk for a while. Robert's admissions about God's work in his life did not have the effect of a magic wand that suddenly took away the problems in their marriage. In fact, the two were still very early in the healing process and had a long way to go. However, they both left this session with renewed hope for their marriage. Because Robert was more willing to accept responsibility for the damage he had caused, he was in a better position to replace the lies he had believed with truth from God. He was surprised, later, to learn that much of the truth he would learn would come as a result of many angry confrontations from Joyce. She was deeply wounded, and the healing would not come easily. But his acceptance of God's speaking to his heart placed him in a solid position to take the difficult steps through the restoration process.

But he had barely begun to see the treacherous path he had followed. It wouldn't be until much later that he would come to fully understand the strength of the lies that he had believed. Nor did he yet fully understand the steps he had taken toward the destruction of his marriage.

A healthy and fulfilling marriage does not just happen. It is a result of hard work and consistent effort. For a husband and wife to fulfill God's design of becoming one flesh, at least two things must be carried out consistently throughout the marriage:

a resistance toward drifting away from the spouse, and a diligent nurturing of the marriage and of each other. People seem to understand that things such as getting an education and managing a career require diligence. Yet many seem to believe that a marriage relationship will blossom naturally and with little effort. Society helps this notion along by creating such myths as, "Everyone has a soul mate, and a good relationship depends on finding this one person," or, "Some marriages were not meant to be, and compatibility is required for a marriage to succeed." These ideas, and others like them, seem to teach that a marriage relationship does not require effort—that it will either work out or it won't.

God's plan for marriage is that it be a wonderful, satisfying relationship in which both parties face life together and enjoy one another. But it is easy to become complacent and fall into a habit of ignoring the relationship, a pattern which is extremely destructive to the marriage. In fact, all that is required in order to render the relationship void of pleasure and satisfaction is to do nothing. When this happens, couples become like a tree limb in a moving body of water. The limb drifts aimlessly along, farther and farther from where it started. Because it expends no effort, it exercises no control over its destination. It is important that both husband and wife work at avoiding the natural tendency to drift away from each other.

The first step in assuring that the couple is continually coming together is for each to value the partner that God has provided specifically for them. Instead of focusing on the perceived flaws in their mate, each spouse needs to decide—and declare—that their mate has value before God and value in the marriage. A wife would pray something like this: *Heavenly Father, I thank You for my husband. I thank You that he is a hard worker and that he loves me. Help me now, Father, to honor and respect him.*

In Robert's case, his first move toward having an affair came long before he ever began the sexual relationship with Teresa. His first step toward sin was that he did not value what God had already given him. He forgot that God had ordained him, as the head of the family, to minister to his wife. Her frustrations and hurts should have been signals to him to stop and take a look at the family. He should have tried to find ways of becoming an encouragement to her and building her up through Christlike service. According to the book of Ephesians, he was to wash his wife with the water of God's Word.[14] Instead, he lied to himself and became convinced that he could find something better elsewhere. He focused on his own wants and needs when he should have been focusing on his wife. If he had done so, he would have made some important realizations. He would have seen how he could have helped her be less frustrated by meeting her emotional needs. And he would have remembered the attributes and characteristics that he once loved. But instead of being grateful for what God had given him, he began to look to the other side of the fence.

The second principle of preserving a marriage is to resist the deceptions that the other side of the fence can offer. It is tempting to believe that other people are not as "human" as the marriage partner. When people are at work, at the gym, or in some other nonhome environment, they do not fully reveal themselves. Their flaws are not as readily seen. When a married person begins to believe that these exterior personalities and behaviors of other people represent a full reality, it can lead to a devaluating of the spouse. That was Robert's second step toward disaster.

At work, he began to notice other women. Because they got up every morning and dressed for success in the workplace, they looked fresh, even sexy. Their makeup and clothes were always tidy. They appeared alluring. He began to deceive himself. He didn't take the time to consider that these same women went home every day and threw on oversized T-shirts and baggy jeans in the comfort of their own homes. He never considered that they, like himself, preferred comfort to professionalism once they left the workplace. He didn't imagine them sleeping in on Saturday morning and waking up with bad breath or even a hangover from an office party the night before. He did not picture them with a sinus infection or a stomach flu. He told himself, *On the other side of the fence, women are always sexy.*

This placed Joyce in a no-win situation. When the two of them dressed up and went somewhere special, he didn't notice. He had already categorized her as less than the best. When she met him at the door with a fresh haircut or a new outfit, he overlooked it. He still saw her negatively. He continued to gather more evidence to substantiate the lie that he was trapped in a lousy marriage.

Women at work spoke to him with respect and deference. He didn't stop to think that this might have something to do with the fact that he was the supervisor of some of them, or that a coworker might have many reasons to ignore his faults and keep him happy. It never occurred to him that the same woman who smiled and complimented him might go home and complain to her husband about his obnoxious attitude. He chose instead to believe that the grass was greener on the other side. He thought, *Other women can see what a great guy I am. Other women appreciate me. Other women respect me the way I deserve to be respected.*

Again, Joyce was in a no-win situation. If she asked him to cut the grass, he saw her as a nag. If she complained that he was not spending enough time at home, he accused her of not appreciating all the hard work he did for the family. Instead of seeking out possible wisdom and truth from his wife, he berated her for not respecting him. Yet when she did compliment him, he found no sense of satisfaction from it. He was using all of his energy wishing for something that didn't exist. Nothing positive she did could measure up to the fantasy of perfection he was creating in his mind.

In order to avoid these pitfalls, it is necessary to nurture the marriage relationship. To do this, it is essential to spend time together. This requires intentional effort to go on regular dates together, to plan a family schedule that includes regular couple time (without the children around), to worship together, and to enter into prayer and Bible study together.

Robert should have used his wandering focus as a warning that he was gradually moving away from his marriage. Instead of taking steps to ensure that he and Joyce spent time together and rebuilt their nurture for one another, he continued to look outside of the relationship for satisfaction. That was his third step toward disaster. He believed the false image he had created. He thought, *How wonderful my life could be if only I could have things my way.*

He assimilated the positives he experienced in his workplace and accepted them as the unwavering standard of how life should be. When Joyce didn't live up to this standard, he convinced himself that she was the problem. He believed that he could have better, and he believed that he *deserved* better. Having saturated himself with this lie, he began to actually court disaster. Until this point, he had only created a sense of dissatisfaction within himself.

Couples who remain faithful to each other safeguard their relationship. They set reasonable boundaries for themselves, making sure that they do not spend undue time with members of the opposite sex. Even happily married couples in fulfilling relationships can be tempted to stray. By making wise decisions, people can protect themselves from temptation. Robert illustrates a person who did not follow this practice. This was his fourth step toward destroying his marriage. He made excursions to the other side of the fence.

At first it seemed innocent enough. Instead of going out to eat with his buddies at lunch, he found reasons to invite one or two female coworkers along. Nothing wrong with that, it seemed. And indeed, often there is nothing wrong with such a situation. What was wrong was his heart. He wanted the company of other women. He wanted to spend time on the other side of the fence. He wanted to feast his eyes on someone whom he found pleasing. He wanted to spend time with someone who found him tough and capable. He started hanging out in areas where there were certain women he found attractive. One or two women especially excited his curiosity. They often made eye contact with him and brushed themselves up against him. They gave him compliments. He started finding reasons to spend time with them after hours. Perhaps he needed help with an account. After working late, he convinced himself it was his duty to spring for drinks or dinner. He discovered that certain women had interests similar to his. *I haven't played tennis in a long time*, he thought. *Surely it would do me good to get out and exercise, wouldn't it?* In this manner, he rationalized many opportunities to spend time on the other side of the fence. He was courting disaster, all the while telling himself that he was just having a little innocent fun.

Meanwhile, he was spending less and less time with Joyce. She was becoming more and more frustrated, but he continued to blame her for their problems. If she were a more understanding wife, he would *want* to spend more time at home, wouldn't he? If she appreciated him the way she should, she would *encourage* him to go out and have a little fun. In his mind, she was just an angry nag. He rarely stopped to consider how his absence placed a heavy burden upon her. He didn't look at the fact that his chasing after a dream was making the realities of her life more difficult. Planning a wedding for their daughter? Her job. Helping their son with college applications? Her job. Cutting the grass? Hire one of the neighbor kids—her job, too. And where was dinner? He had worked all day, and he wanted his rightful meal. And he wanted it served with a smile.

He had completely deluded himself about life on the other side of the fence. In the process, he had deluded himself about life at home as well. It was a short step from there to immorality. It was easy to convince himself that he deserved a little satisfaction in life. Before long, he settled his affections upon one woman. He believed her to be the one for him. This, he believed, was the woman he should have married in the first place. She was exciting, sexy, and encouraging. Because she was part of the lie, she had no faults in his eyes. Because she was trying to keep him happy, she did her best to keep any flaws hidden from him. He rarely saw her without lipstick or perfume. She repeatedly told him what a wonderful man he was and how much she needed him. She fed the lie he wanted to believe, and he began to invest heavily into this new relationship. Rather than providing Joyce with a lifetime of nurture and faithfulness, he was sowing seeds of destruction. He eventually reaped the harvest, taking both Teresa and Joyce into the devastation along with him.

Anger—The First Movement in the Dance

When a marriage has been ravaged by adultery, a great deal of damage has been done to the emotional and spiritual makeup of both spouses. Invariably, the needs of one mate are quite opposite from the needs of the other. The field, therefore, is ripe for conflict. Because emotions at this time are strong and painful, the conflicts that arise are usually volatile. For this reason, marriages that experience adultery usually either end up in divorce or in a state of sustained shutdown.

Couples who divorce follow a predictable route. Argument after argument occurs until one or both spouses exhaust themselves. They finally give up.

Couples who shut down follow a similar pattern. They argue frequently and fail to find healthy resolutions for their conflicts. Eventually they exhaust themselves and give up on the relationship. However, instead of moving toward a dissolution of the marriage, they remain in a relationship that is devoid of emotional intimacy. They live with the absence of Christlike love, which is needed in order to bring encouragement to each other. They are roommates who are cut off from one another, but they lack even the semblance of friendship that roommates often share. A sense of bitterness and resentment keeps the atmosphere tense. They are not divorced, but all ingredients of a healthy marriage have dissolved.

Fortunately, there is another alternative. Couples are not doomed to either divorce court or a wasteland matrimony. Marriages can recover the intimacy of a healthy, growing relationship. But this takes a willingness to work through the painful process of restoration, a course that is rife with obstacles, both expected and unexpected.

People who are struggling to restore their marriages encounter more than the obvious issues. Rebuilding trust, establishing forgiveness, and restoring communication are common themes addressed by therapists. However, other more abstract problems develop along the way that can bewilder and frustrate both the couple and the counselors who work with them. These invisible annoyances spring out of the differing needs of each spouse. In order to adequately address these needs, couples must be willing to work through three areas of difficulty. Because each partner has a specific role in each of these domains, we will consider them as three movements in a carefully choreographed dance.

The three movements of the dance center on opposing needs within the souls of each spouse. We have named these movements expressing anger versus expecting forgiveness, replacing support versus running for cover, and seeking answers versus searching for an end. In order to clearly explain each movement, we have separated them. However, couples should not expect the healing process to proceed in a neatly ordered manner. Many of the steps toward healing are danced simultaneously. For instance, the wronged spouse is likely to experience intense anger throughout the entire process. As the restoration progresses, the intensity and frequency of angry outbursts may lessen. Yet, strong emotion is to be expected throughout the process.

Expressing Anger Versus Expecting Forgiveness

The first movement of the dance of restoration involves a two-phased healing process within the emotions of the injured spouse. He or she experiences a wide range of emotions, vacillating between a desperate desire to save the marriage and a furious rage toward the adulterous spouse (and sometimes the extramarital partner).

Stage one is filled with fluctuation between anger and desperation. When the affair is first uncovered, the initial reaction is usually shock and anger. But after the first onslaught of intensity subsides, a person begins to feel the weight of the potential loss of the marriage and may become anxious to save it. This desire can come for many reasons: love for the straying spouse, financial dependence, avoidance of loss, a potential disruption of lifestyle, embarrassment, fear of change, concerns about the children involved, family values, or religious convictions. Most experience a combination of these, but often, they cannot explain them clearly, other than to say, "I'll do whatever it takes to save the marriage."[15]

At some point, usually after counseling has begun, the betrayed spouse moves into stage two of healing: prolonged anger. This often occurs at a surprising time, usually after the errant spouse repents and begins to work on the relationship. The betrayed spouse then relaxes his or her grip on saving the marriage and experiences a return of the intense anger.

These two stages (vacillation and prolonged anger), both take place within the emotions of the spouse. However, they cause confusion and pain within the repentant spouse whose desire is for understanding and forgiveness.

Joyce and Robert have arrived at this juncture. Joyce needs to express her anger. Robert desires to be forgiven and understood. Clashes are inevitable.

After Joyce and Robert had been attending counseling for about two months, Robert privately expressed frustration to Andy. "I thought that once I broke up with Teresa, Joyce would stop being so angry."

"Sometimes it's not that easy."

"I don't understand what Joyce wants from me. When she first found out about the affair, she was so mad that she threw stuff across the room! But since then, I thought things were getting better."

"Things don't seem better now?"

"Two weeks ago she said she forgave me. But now I can't please her. Nothing I do is right. She blames the whole affair on me. She blames all of our marriage problems on me. If the cat sneezes, she blames that on me, too."

Andy and Robert talked for a few minutes about Robert's comments. Andy pointed out that Joyce is correct to blame the whole affair on Robert.

"Joyce did not make the choice for you to stray. That choice was yours alone."

"But she's not perfect, either. Our marriage wasn't exactly ideal before I had the affair."

"That's probably true. But your infidelity has opened a depth of pain that wasn't present before. The problems that existed prior to the affair have been exacerbated. Unfortunately, by committing an act of betrayal, you've temporarily disqualified yourself from addressing the pre-affair marital problems. Right now, you have to bear the burden of the anger that you have incited. Later, after Joyce has had time to heal, there will be time to work on other areas in the marriage. For now, your job is to do everything you can to accept responsibility for the pain and anger you have brought to Joyce and to do whatever you can to reinstate trust into the relationship."

"But how could she be so forgiving on some days, and so angry on others? I never know what to expect."

"I know that this is difficult," Andy replied, "but it is also normal."

"Normal? I feel like it's all just crazy. Now that I'm coming home every night and trying to be a good husband, she hates my guts. It's not fair. When I was doing the wrong thing, she loved me. Now that I'm doing the right thing, she hates me. I don't know how to fix it."

"I don't think Joyce loved you *more* for doing wrong. She was just working hard to save the relationship. Now that you are investing into the relationship, she is relaxing. Her feelings are now free to come to the surface. And remember, you have known the details of the affair for a long time. Much of what is being revealed to Joyce is new information. She needs time to react and respond to the things she is learning."

"I guess that makes sense. It's just so unpredictable."

"Well, it might seem crazy and unpredictable to you right now. But it makes perfect sense to Joyce. If you compare her trust to a rabbit venturing from its burrow, it will seem more logical to you, as well."

Robert gave Andy a quizzical look. "I don't get it."

"Joyce is wounded, and she's mad about it. Her emotions are probably stronger than she's ever experienced before. She doesn't know what to do with them. At the same time, she has a strong desire to rebuild the trust she once had in you. So she ventures out of her burrow and tries to love you, but she feels vulnerable when she does. At first sight of anything that stirs her fears, she darts back inside to safety. Anger, or emotional distance, returns."[16]

Andy and Robert talked for a few minutes. Then Andy invited Joyce to join the session.

"Robert says you're pretty angry with him."

"I keep thinking about the two of them together at the lake. I can't get that picture out of my head," said Joyce. "I thought I had dealt with it, but I guess not."

"When that picture comes back into your mind, how does that make you feel?"

"Angry," she choked on the word. Taking a deep breath, she continued. "I'm not angry all the time. But sometimes—" she fought for composure. "Sometimes I'm so furious that I can't believe it myself. It's almost overwhelming."

"Let's talk about your anger. What seems to ignite it for you?"

"Robert has absolutely no idea how much he has hurt me." Her words were low and controlled, as though they were attack dogs straining to be unleashed. She paused, faced Robert, and let go.

"How could you hurt me like this? I'll never be able to trust you again. I hate you! I hate what you've done to me!"

"You see?" Robert said to Andy. "You see what I'm talking about? I can't live like this."

"*You* can't live like this?" Joyce sputtered her disgust. "I don't even know why I came here today. At night I fight to fall asleep because I can't get the thought of you and that woman out of my head. Every morning I wake up and want to scream at you, because I remember some lie you told."

"I can't pay for this mistake for the rest of my life!" Robert exclaimed.

"*You* can't pay for this mistake? What about the price I have to pay? Do you realize how many times you told me that all the problems in our marriage were because of *my* suspicious nature?" Joyce was beginning to shout. "You told me I was paranoid! You made me feel like I was going crazy! AND I WAS RIGHT ALL THE TIME!"

"I can't go back into the past and fix this. I wish I could, but I can't. But I've got to tell you, sometimes I'm about ready to give up."

Andy surprised Robert by saying that many couples do choose to give up at this point. But then he gave the couple some hope. He explained that they were experiencing a common pattern of recuperation from infidelity.

"As Joyce experiences this anger," he explained, "it must be seen as a stage in healing the marriage. It doesn't have to be the end of the marriage. It's a part of the restoration process. As long as Joyce was the one carrying the burden of trying to make the marriage work, she was not free to express her anger. But when you, Robert, began to take on a greater responsibility for the marriage, Joyce no longer had to carry the burden. She let it go. When she did, her buried feelings surfaced. Robert, if you will allow your wife to express her anger to you, she will get beyond it. Then you will be able to jointly work on the marriage. I warn you though—this is an extremely difficult process. It will take both courage and humility."

At Andy's suggestion, Joyce made several appointments to come in alone so that she could work on ridding herself of the terrible weight of the anger she was carrying. She learned it was not necessary for her to express all of her anger to Robert, and that it was not wise to use language and words that she might later regret.

"Both of you will get beyond this," said Andy. "And the less damage done, the better."

In a later session, Andy encouraged Robert to remain faithful to his commitment to help Joyce by accepting her anger. "Remember that as you allow Joyce to express her feelings, you are also allowing God to work deep repentance in you. God is working in you to transform you into the husband and person that He has called you to be."

Joyce and Robert agreed that they would need outside help to get through this painful time in the restoration of their marriage. They were glad they had chosen to seek out counseling.[17]

Our couple has now entered the process of *expressing anger versus expecting forgiveness*. Most couples are surprised to discover that the conflict they are experiencing is a vitally important part of moving toward restoration. They are often relieved to learn that vacillation between forgiveness and intense anger is not uncommon.

Stage One: Vacillation between Anger and Wanting to Save the Marriage. This stage may actually begin before the affair is finally admitted. When a spouse begins to suspect an affair, strong emotions (fear, anger, and worry) swirl within. Instinctively, many want the marriage to work. Therefore, energy is expended in a back-and-forth struggle between attempting to confirm suspicions and attempting to entice the wayward spouse to stay in the marriage. After the affair is confirmed, this vacillation may continue, but at a greater intensity. Fear gives way to shock. Anger gives way to rage. Worry gives way to desperation.

In the early days after the discovery, the injured spouse may offer forgiveness and move into a period of trying to be a better husband or wife in order to hold on to the one who has strayed. Questions such as, "What did I do to push you away?" or, "Where did I fail you?" are often asked. (Wives, especially, tend to search the marriage to find their own faults.) However, the vacillation and attempt at self-improvement usually give way to a strong undercurrent of anger.

Stage Two: Prolonged Anger. As Joyce worked harder and harder to improve herself and fix the marriage, she began to become overwhelmed with negative emotions. Feelings of hurt, betrayal, mistrust, and anger churned within her like a hot boiler ready to explode. At this point, many betrayed spouses withdraw from these feelings and enter into an "I-don't-care" ambivalence about the marriage—and about life in general. However, when couples undergo counseling, the movement toward healing the relationship causes the wronged spouse to face his or her emotions. A return of intense anger usually results.

The Returning Anger

Why does the anger return? Typically, the anger has been stifled until this point, but it is still present and ready to burst out. Although most people experience an initial explosion of anger, they sometimes shut down their feelings almost immediately in order to save the marriage. For example, a woman who has suspected an affair and has worked hard to get her husband to give up his mistress would not risk it all by saying that she will never love him again. But as he begins to show that he is willing to be faithful, this strong emotion on her part is likely to surface. Other times, people subdue their emotions because they are overwhelmed by their feelings and do not know how to handle them. But eventually these strong feelings refuse to be ignored.

Another reason the betrayed spouse returns to anger is the discovery of more information. For example, when couples go to therapy, the anger has usually cooled and both are there to work on the marriage. But throughout the therapy, the offending spouse is encouraged to give full disclosure, as the faithful spouse demands it. New information is revealed. Perhaps the offending spouse confesses that the affair occurred over a longer period of time than was initially admitted. Maybe there has been more than one lover. Sometimes the loss of money is discovered, or the betrayer will admit to giving away an item that he or she had earlier denied. At times there is a realization that the lover was brought into the house. These and other discoveries can easily cause a return of pain and anger.

When anger revisits the relationship, the repentant spouse is quite often surprised. They do not know how to handle the fury that suddenly bursts open. There has been a belief that things have been going well in the reconciliation. They think that forgiveness has already been extended and that angry words are no longer necessary. They usually react defensively, saying something like, "We've covered all this before. I can't go back and change the past. Why can't we just move on?" Bewilderment, frustration, and hopelessness are all common responses.[18]

It is important for the adulterous spouse to realize that their mate must be given the freedom to be angry. It is necessary to move through this anger in order for genuine reconciliation to occur. This period is frightening because it is intense and usually involves severe words. However, the anger is temporary. When given liberty to express these strong feelings, the spouse will usually move beyond them. Bitterness and resentment will not take root, and together the couple can rebuild intimacy.

The Intensity of the Anger

In addition to understanding why the anger returns, it is also helpful to understand why the anger is intense. First, the feelings of betrayal and the loss of trust are extremely damaging. A person's soul mate has destroyed the foundational elements for a secure marriage.

Second, betrayal is an assault upon God's design for marriage. Though the individuals may not realize it, much damage has been done to the spiritual framework of their marriage.

One of the God-given roles of a wife is to respect her husband. When she is the offender, she has damaged the esteem that God designed her to buttress.[19] Rebuilding his sense of respect and self-esteem becomes her great task when restoring the marriage.

When the offender is the husband, he, too, has acted in a manner that is specifically opposite from his God-given role in the marriage. He has brought destruction to his wife, when his biblical responsibility is to bring life, health, and security to her.[20]

In addition, the man has been given a stronger command by God to act as the spiritual protector in the relationship. The Scriptures identify the wife as the "weaker vessel."[21] One way to understand this passage is to see her as the more vulnerable of the two in the relationship. Although she is just as capable and intelligent as her husband, she has been charged with the task of yielding to his leadership and submitting to his authority. This requires a great deal of selflessness and sacrifice on her part. It places her in a vulnerable position in the marriage. If she has attempted to faithfully carry out this role, her self-sacrifice, which God has commanded be considered and honored, has instead been trampled upon by the betrayal.

Third, if the affair had been suspected before it was finally out in the open, the faithful spouse usually incurred a great deal of emotional damage during the discovery process. The admission of the affair, then, serves to shine a light that exposes a multitude of offenses. The wronged spouse begins to realize the game of deception that has been played. They may have made many attempts to discuss it, perhaps even by asking specific questions such as, "Are you having an affair?" Typically, an adulterer responds to these attempts by attacks and blame-casting. They may point to their own trustworthiness and accuse the mate of being suspicious or ungodly. During this period of time, the self-esteem and self-trust of the faithful spouse are severely attacked.

Women are especially vulnerable to this kind of assault. When a husband tells his wife that she is crazy, she doubts herself and her own God-given intuition. She blames herself for her suspicions and assumes that her husband's lack of interest in sex means that she is no longer appealing. (Even if the frequency of sexual activity did not change during the affair, wives berate themselves for "not being enough" to satisfy their husbands sexually.) It is difficult to exaggerate the damage this causes to the spirit of a wife.

Regardless of which spouse is the offender, once the affair is discovered, the innocent spouse realizes that not only has betrayal occurred, but personal attacks and deliberate denigration have also taken place. The adulterous spouse knowingly allowed the innocent mate to believe he or she were inept and unworthy of affection. The offender knew of the confusion and still allowed the destruction of spirit, so that the fantasy and excitement of the illicit relationship could continue. Complicating matters is that this damaging behavior is usually a repeated cycle, which exhausts and destroys the spirit of the faithful spouse. When they begin to remember past conversations and realize the attack that took place on their spirit, the level of hurt is almost unfathomable. The rift in these situations is deep. Many counseling sessions are spent dealing with the pain it causes.

Finally, there was often anger present in the marriage before the affair was ever discovered. When a person cheats, they throw fuel on a smoldering fire. Unfortunately, it is not appropriate to say, "This anger has to do with the affair and I'll accept it, but that anger comes from somewhere else so I can defend myself." There must be full acceptance for the heat that has been fueled. Later, when the marriage has been largely restored, both the husband and wife can explore the condition of the marriage that existed before the affair and attempt to resolve the difficulties that were present. But until that time, the offending spouse must bear the weight of the anger.

Principles for Counselors

The stage of prolonged anger is precarious for counselors and pastors who mentor the couple. On the one hand, there is a danger that the wounded spouse may get stuck in anger and bitterness. On the other hand, there is the danger of passing through this phase too quickly. If the wronged spouse is rushed, the Holy Spirit is not given sufficient time to work within the person's heart. This may result in feelings of false guilt that will stifle the healing process. There are several principles for the counselor to keep in mind that will help keep these two opposing dangers in clear view.

1. **Scripture indicates that there are times for righteous anger.** Adultery is one of these times. God sets the example throughout the Old Testament when He speaks of His grief and anger over Israel's rebellion against Him. One might argue, "But God paid the ultimate price by giving His own Son for the forgiveness of this adultery." This is absolutely true. In fact, it is this sacrifice that will eventually enable forgiveness to occur. But our heavenly Father allowed Himself centuries of patience, anger, discipline, and a general working out of His plan of redemption. The adultery that ultimately began in the Garden of Eden (when mankind chose his own way instead of God's way) was brought to restoration through a process that took centuries. God did not hurry Himself, and we should not hurry the injured partner. The anger is justifiable. In fact, it is in agreement with the anger of God.[22] So, time must be allowed for the wounded spouse to adjust to the intense waves of emotion that surge within.

2. **It is important to maintain the proper perspective.** Affairs rarely occur in healthy, happy marriages. Usually, counselors can quickly see some of the problems that were present before the affair occurred. Often the faithful spouse contributed equally to these problems. The counselor must resist the temptation to address these problems too soon after the counseling has begun. The affair has caused devastation to the marriage, and it must remain the first priority until significant healing has taken place. Other issues can eventually be addressed, but only after the destruction caused by the affair has been dealt with thoroughly.

One way to understand this concept is to picture the marriage as a house. Within this house were many areas that needed repair. The roof leaked. The foundation shifted. The plumbing was bad. Both the husband and the wife were at fault for the poor condition of the house. But one day, while one spouse was napping inside, the other poured gasoline all over the house and lit a match. The condition of the home has now reached a new level of destruction, and the faithful spouse has been badly burned.

It is the role of the Holy Spirit—through God's Word, a godly counselor, and the repentant spouse—to bring healing to the injured person. The offender must begin to clean up the rubble that has been created. It is senseless for the offender to complain about the leaky roof of a house that they have destroyed. It is offensive to say, "Well, I know I burned down the house, but can't we just forget about that? I mean, after all, the plumbing wasn't any good. That was your fault." With the counselor's help, both the husband and the wife must look at the destruction that has occurred. Then the offender must be willing to pace the rebuilding process according to the needs of their mate.

Once the ashes have been cleared and the salve of restoration, repentance, and the rebuilding of trust have brought a degree of healing to the wounded soul of the faithful spouse, the process of rebuilding the house can be addressed. That is the time to talk about the causes of the "leaky roof, horrible plumbing, and shifting foundation" that had existed before the fire. These pre-affair problems do need to be addressed eventually, so that a healthy relationship can fully be restored. But they need to be addressed in their proper priority.

3. **It is possible for the wounded spouse to remain bitter.** The role of the counselor is to help a person identify and express his or her anger. Sufficient time must be allowed for this process. But it is also the role of the counselor to help move a person through the anger and onward toward healing. How will the counselor know if a confrontation is necessary to aid in dispelling the anger? First, much time must be spent in prayer seeking the

guidance of the Holy Spirit. Second, there are a number of clues that will raise a warning flag:

a. In spite of the consistent, honest attempts of the repentant spouse, months pass, and the wronged spouse continues to hurl anger without any period of relief, distraction, or hope.

b. In spite of the consistent, honest attempts of the repentant spouse, other stages of the dance of restoration are not entered.

c. After allowing sufficient time for the initial shock and anger to wear off, the faithful spouse refuses to grant any encouragement or acknowledge the honest attempts to restore the marriage.

d. After allowing sufficient time for the initial shock and anger to wear off, the faithful spouse is reluctant to pray, read the Bible, attend church, or do homework assignments given by the counselor.[23]

The issue of bitterness needs careful handling. If the couple is early in the process of restoration, the counselor should not urge the wounded spouse toward forgiveness. But if the couple seems to have passed significantly through the other two movements (*rebuilding support versus running for cover* and *seeking answers versus searching for an end*) without a reduction in the intensity of the anger, then the counselor may need to help the wounded spouse to forgive and enter into spiritual healing.

Anger toward the Third Party

Sometimes the wounded spouse expresses anger toward the third party during arguments. For example, when a wife has been betrayed, she might call the other woman names and even make threats against her. Because the husband has been emotionally involved with this woman, his instinctive reaction is to defend her honor. This is a mistake.

The role of the offender is not to defend the adulterous lover, but to restore trust and love in the marriage. Defending the former lover needs to be avoided at all cost. The more a person can agree with their spouse, the sooner trust will be restored. For example, if a betrayed husband asks, "How could you have anything to do with that jerk?" his wife should not respond, "He's not a jerk. He's actually a pretty nice guy." This will only instill insecurity within the husband. A better response would be, "I don't know. I wasn't thinking clearly. I was wrong. I should have remained faithful to you. God has given me all I need in you, and I was crazy to try to find His good gifts anywhere else." This kind of a response will go a long way toward rebuilding the trust.

On occasion, an injured spouse moves beyond hurling insults to making threats. Even in these instances, defending the former lover can still be avoided. For example, a betrayed wife might say, "I'm going to go beat up that witch and tear every hair out of her head." Her husband should not respond, "Don't you touch her. She isn't as bad as you think." That kind of response will cause the spouse to continue to feel as though they are the second choice. Loyalties will not appear to have returned to the marriage, but instead appear to remain with the third party.

A better response would be, "I don't blame you for being so angry at her. I gave to her what I should have been giving to you. I hope you won't really go confront her, because I would be afraid of what might happen. The police might get involved, or you might get hurt or go to jail. I've already caused you so much pain. I don't want to see you go through any more." That kind of response helps to prove that loyalties have returned to the marriage. The concern is for the safety and healing of the marriage partner, not for the one who represents such a tremendous threat to the security of the marriage.

Most spouses will not actually do violence. Usually, they are simply expressing their anger. Sometimes they are testing their mates to find out where their loyalties lie. If the repentant spouse does not defend the former lover, then maturity and spirituality usually take over and the threatened actions are not taken. (There are times that threats are serious. If a person has reason to believe that violence might actually take place, they need to immediately contact the professional who is working with their specific situation and seek direction.)

On the other hand, the offended spouse needs to remember that anger is best directed toward the right person. It is not healthy to blame the third party for the affair. A little venting toward this person is understandable and natural. However, the focus of attention should remain on the spouse who strayed. He or she is the person who violated the marriage. For this reason, we do not usually recommend that the offended spouse talk to or confront the third person. Many times, this person will lie and exaggerate the depth of the affair. This is counterproductive to healing.

What should take place if the other man or woman was a friend before the affair? Sometimes the wounded party desires to confront this friend because the betrayal is so painful. Of course, this is an instance where some of the anger is reasonably directed toward the former friend. Even so, the blame should be for a friendship betrayed, not for a marriage destroyed. Any anger for disruption to the marriage should be aimed toward the cheating spouse.[24]

Another important principle concerning the third party is that the offending spouse usually does not have negative feelings toward their extramarital partner. Sometimes the faithful spouse becomes angry because their mate will not join in expressing blame toward or angry feelings about the other person. Asking for these feelings is counterproductive and unnecessary. While the repentant spouse need not defend the former lover, they are not required to develop hatred or other negative feelings. This is not needed for the marriage to heal and should be left alone.

Contrasting Needs

A final area of concern in relation to anger concerns the contrasting need of the repentant spouse. When a person admits to having an affair, their strongest hope is to be forgiven. This desire is understandable. All people seek to be relieved from the weight of guilt that sin brings. However, premature forgiveness can stifle the restoration of the healing process for both parties. The offended party needs to unpack his or her anger so that when forgiveness is finally offered, it is fully and freely given.

This sets up an agonizing set of circumstances for the offender. The betrayed spouse is intensely angry. It is not realistic to expect this anger to be expressed coolly and carefully.[25] On the other hand, a person who has repented and is attempting to restore the marital relationship has been carrying a burden of guilt. Now, in addition to this guilt, this person is faced with an incredible load of anger directed at them in a fierce manner and on a daily basis. This can seem unbearable at times. The natural tendency is to give up and leave. If the marriage is to be fully restored, the offending spouse is going to need some encouragement during this process. There are several suggestions for obtaining this encouragement and gaining the stamina needed during these difficult days.

1. First, the adulterous spouse needs to seek forgiveness from God. God has already sent His Son, Jesus, to pay the penalty for all of our sins. God's wrath has already been spent upon Christ's cross. Therefore, unlike the wounded spouse, God is ready and able to forgive at the moment of repentance. A genuine

prayer to God agreeing with Him about the grievous nature of adultery and a sincere request for forgiveness is the first step toward meeting this need in the life of the offending spouse.[26]

2. Second, he or she needs to participate in counseling to restore the marriage. Whereas the injured spouse may not always be emotionally strong enough to encourage him, a counselor will see the efforts and improvements. Positive feedback from a therapist or godly leader can provide the necessary encouragement and give hope that restoration can occur in time.

3. Third, the offending spouse can meet this need by seeking restoration with their church family. If the person was already a member, meeting with the pastor can be a means of establishing a support system.

Scripture teaches us to allow the older believers to teach the younger believers. It also states that as iron sharpens iron, so one person sharpens another.[27] This means that as we spend time with one another in open, honest relationships, we help one another improve in our lives. Finding an older Christian whom one respects and trusts is a good way to gain support. The mentor can pray with and listen to the repentant spouse, as well as hold them accountable for sticking to new commitments. This can be a great source of encouragement.

If the person was not active in a church family, they need to find a church home. Then, a private consultation with a member of the ministerial staff might be helpful. Even if the repentant spouse decides not to confide the circumstances of the marriage, they can request discipleship, which includes a manner of being taught about the way to live life according to God's plan.

In either circumstance (whether one is already active in a church or not), it is important that these conversations be held with mature, trusted ministers. It is also important that confidentiality be respected. It is not necessary for the sinful behavior to be discussed with other church members, or even other members of the church staff. Even if resignation from leadership positions needs to be made, this can be done without explanation of the sinful circumstance that led to the resignation of the post.[28]

4. Finally, the offended spouse can play a role in supporting the repentant spouse. Although anger is justifiable and even necessary for healing, the wronged party can learn to be a source of encouragement even while angry. This may seem to be a contradiction, but learning to encourage in the midst of pain can be an important part of spiritual growth and emotional restoration. This can be done through simple acknowledgments of the efforts made by the repentant spouse. The following are some examples:

> "I know that I have been very angry with you lately. In fact, I'm still mad, but I want you to know that I'm glad you have been willing to listen to what I have been saying. I'm sure it hasn't been easy."

> "The other day, you tried really hard to tell me how you were feeling. Thanks for trying."

> "Thanks for going to talk to our pastor about our problems. It gives me some hope that things will work out."

Another way the wounded spouse can give encouragement is to attempt to answer the repentant spouse's questions about progress. This is especially important when the offending spouse is the man. Most husbands ask for a concrete time frame and for a measurable progress report. They will ask such things as, "How long are you going to be angry?" "Are you feeling 30 percent better or 80 percent better?" "On a scale of 1 to 10, how angry are you today?" Often the wife will see this as an attempt to minimize the damage he has done to her, and she will respond with anger. It is helpful to realize that this is not an attempt to minimize, but a desire to overcome frustration. It is a normal response to stressful emotional conflict.

This type of question is a signal that the offending spouse needs hope. It is important to try to respond to these questions, although it may not be possible to give specific numerical answers. One way to do this is to focus on what has been accomplished so far in the process.

For example, wounded spouses sometimes speak of their lives as a large puzzle with pieces that are missing. Healing becomes a process of finding the missing pieces. When asked for a progress report, the angry spouse can think about the parts of the puzzle that are complete so far. They can say, "Well, last Saturday we had a good day. I didn't think about it all day. Not until midnight when I woke up did I think about the affair," or, "I can see how some things have improved. For instance, you are coming home earlier from the office, and that makes me feel secure that you aren't with someone else." Even though a numerical answer is not being given, a reply containing specific information helps the repentant spouse to know the relationship is progressing.

Robert and Joyce struggled with their contrasting needs of expressing anger and expecting forgiveness throughout the restoration process. As Robert stopped expecting Joyce to forgive him and instead gave her the freedom to express her anger, she gradually began to develop trust in the sincerity of his repentance. However, as the dance of restoration continued, they ran into more areas of conflicting needs.

5

The Dance
Continues

Replacing Support Versus Running for Cover

The second movement in the dance of restoration addresses the conflicting needs of *replacing support versus running for cover*. Whereas the perpetrator would very much like to keep sinful behavior a private issue, the desire of the wounded spouse is the exact opposite. This person has a need to replace the support system that has been lost from the marriage.

Robert and Joyce have danced their way into this movement. In order to fill the void that Robert caused with his betrayal, Joyce began to talk about it with her friends and family. This caused embarrassment to her husband and introduced more resentment into the relationship.

"I don't understand why Joyce has to go around telling our business to the whole world," Robert complained. "It's private."

"Joyce needs support right now," Andy explained.

"But I don't want everyone in town to know what has happened. Now that I've stopped the affair, I want to put it all behind me. But Joyce won't allow it. She throws it in my face constantly. Then she talks to other people behind my back. My reputation is ruined."

"Believe me, the last thing on my mind right now is saving your reputation!" Joyce spat angrily.

"Well, that seems rather obvious," Robert shot back.

Andy allowed them to argue for a while. Then he broke in with some insights. "What you are experiencing is to be expected right now. Your needs are the exact opposite from each other's. Robert, I'm afraid you are going to have to be the one to bear the weight of the conflict, but there are a few things that Joyce can do to help."

"It doesn't seem fair that she gets to have her needs met, but I don't get to have mine met," said Robert. "I know I'm the one who had the affair, but Joyce is no angel. She has her faults, too."

Andy was direct. "Yes, Robert, you will both have to make sacrifices in order to save this marriage. But you have to remember that you have already made the choice to meet your own needs at her expense. If you continue to meet your needs at her expense, you will prevent her from healing. If she does not heal from the wounds you have inflicted upon her, you will never have a healthy and satisfying relationship with her."

"But I didn't think that anyone else could be responsible for her healing other than herself. How can I be responsible for her choices?"

"You can't be responsible for her choices. You can only be responsible for your own choices. Joyce can certainly obtain healing by herself. She and God can do all of the work that is necessary for her healing. But if she is to heal toward the marriage, and toward reconciling with you, you have to be consistent in your faithfulness to love her sacrificially. You have to be willing to nurture her. And you have to be willing to put aside some of your own needs to meet hers. These are some of the choices you will have to make if you want the marriage to heal."

"You see, Robert, when betrayal has occurred in a marriage, the husband and wife each has differing needs. The repentant spouse has a need for privacy and confidentiality. But the betrayed spouse needs the support of friends. Before Joyce ever knew about you and Teresa, you had been struggling with the hurt of your decisions for quite some time. Joyce had not. She just found out about this, and the revelation has devastated her. She cannot put it behind her yet. She must talk about it in order to face it and heal from it. She has to have friends in whom she can confide. If Joyce is to heal from her trauma, you must yield to her need."

Andy shifted his focus to Joyce, who was looking a little triumphant by this time. "Joyce," he said. "Are you still willing to work toward healing this marriage?"

"Yes. I'm not sure why, but I guess I'm still willing to work on it."

"Good. I'm glad to hear that," Andy replied. He went on to encourage Joyce to continue to seek support from her friends and talk with others about her feelings and struggles.

"But remember," he continued, "after you and Robert get beyond this to the point of complete reconciliation, you are going to want to go on with the rest of your lives. If you choose to talk about your problems with too many people, you are giving them the opportunity to gossip about you and Robert. Right now you need support. But you are also going to eventually want to put it behind you. You aren't going to want to face it every day. That will be a difficult thing to do if a lot of people know about your present difficulties." Andy went on to recommend that she select one or two friends in whom she could confide. These trusted friends should be people who would not betray her confidence and who would be willing to walk with her through her healing process. He cautioned her not to choose family members for this task.

"Family members tend to take sides," he said. "And family members have difficulty forgetting. If you expose your hurt to your family, it is likely they will hold this against Robert indefinitely. It would be very difficult to restore your marriage with that kind of pressure."

By the end of the session, Robert and Joyce began to see the wisdom in Andy's words.

"You've mentioned to me before that all of this is new to Joyce," said Robert. "I've been wanting to—you know—run for cover, so to speak. But I guess she kind of feels like her whole world has been turned upside down. I see now that she's not trying to get even with me. She needs support from her friends."

Joyce was shocked at Robert's admission of her needs. For the first time in weeks, her face softened, and her voice lost some of its edge. "Yes," she said. "I do need support, but I guess you're right about being selective. I don't want the whole town whispering about our problems once I'm ready to forget them. I do have a best friend I can trust. And there is a lady at church who will pray with me if I ask her."

"That's good," said Andy. "And don't forget, your sessions here are going to be a valuable outlet for you, as well. You aren't alone in this."

Joyce and Robert both went home feeling they had made some progress in understanding one another that day. But each knew they still had a long way to go.

Embarrassment and shame accompany most sin. It takes a great deal of humility and brokenness to admit wrongdoing, especially if harm has been caused to someone else. It is this shame and discomfort that causes the offending spouse to desire privacy. Typically, the offender has been in turmoil for some time. They have spent a great deal of energy attempting to hide the infidelity and manage the guilt it has brought. There was excitement at the beginning of the extramarital relationship, but the drawbacks eventually began to siphon away the fun. The adulterer then began to function as a dolphin caught in a shrimp net, expending large amounts of energy, but remaining trapped. By the time the betrayal is finally discovered, there is a sense of relief. The discovery does not bring happiness, but the weight of secrecy and entanglement is lifted.

Once the affair is ended, the adulterer wants to forget it ever happened. There is regret for prior decisions and a desire to return to a peaceful life. The embarrassment of the infidelity is something they want to place in the past. But this desire collides with the needs of the betrayed spouse.

When betrayal is discovered, life seems to implode. Marriage, the most trusted relationship, has crumbled. A home once believed to be stable and secure has collapsed. A whirlwind of powerful, unexpected emotion seems to completely overwhelm. The burden is much too great to bear alone. Emotional intimacy has been lost, and there is a desire to fill the void by talking, talking, and talking about the situation. Trusted confidants are needed to help carry the load.[29]

The need for support, especially prayer support, is real and legitimate. Indeed, the Scriptures urge us to bear one another's burdens.[30] Talking about pain brings about temporary release. At least in the short term, the burden seems lighter because someone is sympathetic and caring. A feeling of injustice finds an understanding ear. But because there is incredible anger, there is also little concern about the adulterer's desire for privacy.

This conflict of needs sometimes results in a new kind of attack on the betrayed spouse. Even a truly repentant person may launch this attack because of a desire for confidentiality. They will say that it is wrong to tell friends about their problem. Accusations of gossip will be made when pain is discussed with friends or family. If a pastor is consulted, the adulterer becomes indignant because of the reputation that has been "ruined" in the eyes of a respected person.

Without meaning to, the adulterer is working to shut down his or her spouse. The motives are not from an attempt to lie, as they had been in the past. Nonetheless, this is still an attempt to shut down the spouse. Before everything was out in the open, a great deal of energy was expended in attempts to deny and cover up the affair. Now that the truth about the affair is known, there is a desire to avoid embarrassment and keep the honor of the family's name.

Is there an answer to this dilemma? The good news is that there is a way to resolve this conflict of needs—to a point. This resolution calls upon both spouses to make some adjustments, but the offender must carry the primary responsibility to adjust. Their duty is to lay aside personal needs in favor of the wounded spouse. At first this may seem unfair. However, the underlying truth is that the betrayer is the cause of the dilemma. Regardless of the state of the marriage before the infidelity occurred, the conflict of needs at this point in the marriage is a direct result of the extramarital affair. As harsh of a judgment as it may seem, the adulterer chose to meet their own needs at the expense of their spouse. Now, if the marriage is to be restored, that must be reversed. The offender must be willing to yield to the needs of their mate. However, a word of caution also needs to be given to the betrayed spouse.

It is important to be selective in choosing a support system. Talking to all of one's friends and family members about the unfaithfulness may bring negative returns. As difficult as it may be to believe at this stage, they will eventually be ready to move beyond the crisis of betrayal and desire to walk through life with a restored marriage. However, marital affairs are titillating. They are the story lines for best-selling novels and TV dramas. It is human nature, even among friends, to remember and discuss the dramatic facts of other people's lives. There is a need to find support—but wisdom must be exercised when seeking support from others. Support and encouragement bring life, but gossip and revenge bring death to a relationship. Nothing is gained by telling *all* of one's friends and family members. Indiscriminate venting may plant seeds of destruction within the foundation of restoration. It is important to carefully select persons on which to lean during this time. Only a few trusted confidants are necessary to create the needed support system. A pastor or counselor can also be an important source of help. Selective choosing during this phase will help to establish the circumstances necessary for the betrayed spouse to move forward.

A final word of caution is needed here. We strongly recommend that these confidants be persons outside of the family.

Family members are devoted for life. They are also around at times of celebration and tradition. When the traumatized couple is ready to forgive and move on, family members may not be. They will still remember and may even throw obstacles into the path of healing because of their own hurt and anger toward the repentant spouse. If this occurs, then occasions meant for celebration may instead become significant reminders of a painful past.

Seeking Answers Versus Searching for an End

The final movement in the dance of restoration involves the conflicting needs of *seeking answers versus searching for an end*. As we have already pointed out, the offender has a strong desire to forget the betrayal by placing it in the past and keeping it there. They would like to bring the restoration process to an end and go on with life. However, the wounded spouse has just experienced an emotional unraveling resulting in a multitude of questions that must be answered. This requires that the betrayal be discussed, something the repentant spouse would rather not do. Robert and Joyce have encountered this stage on their path to restoration.

"We seem to be going around in circles," Robert complained. "She keeps asking me the same questions over and over. I try to answer her, but nothing seems to satisfy."

"Well, he doesn't answer my questions," said Joyce. "All he says is, 'I don't know,' or, 'I don't think you really want to know the answer to that,' or, 'Can we please drop this?' He never really tells me anything."

"I want to go on with our marriage. I don't see that it is necessary for me to relive every step of the affair. I want to do like the Bible says and forget what lies behind and go on toward what lies ahead."[31]

"Robert," said Andy. "I think Joyce wants the same thing." Joyce nodded in agreement. "When we feel betrayed, we are filled with questions and insecurities. Asking these questions will help Joyce to leave her insecurities and mistrust behind. If you prove that you no longer have anything to hide from her, then she will begin to develop security in the marriage."

"But I do try to answer her questions. She's not satisfied with my answers."

"Some questions don't have answers. But if you are transparent with her and tell her what you were thinking and feeling at the time, it should be sufficient."

"I don't understand what you mean."

"What is one question Joyce asks?"

"Yesterday, she kept asking me if it was her fault that I had the affair."

"How did you respond?"

"I told her, no. It wasn't her fault."

"And?"

"And then she said, 'Well, why did you need her, then?' I said, 'I didn't need her.' Then she asked me, 'So, why did you do it?' All I could say was, 'I don't know.' And that's the truth. I don't know why I did it."

"This is the point at which you need to be transparent. You don't know the factual reasons, so you can't give them to Joyce. But you can tell her what you were feeling at the time of the betrayal. What were some of the feelings you were experiencing at the time you got involved with Teresa?"

"Well, I felt very alone. Joyce got a promotion on her job, and it required more time from her than it used to. The kids had both moved out, and I was coming home to an empty house. I guess I was lonely."

"So, you are saying it was my fault!" said Joyce defensively.

"No. I'm not saying that at all!"

"Well, what are you saying, then?"

After allowing the couple to volley back and forth for a while, Andy shed some light on the issue.

"Joyce, let's look at Robert's reply. He has explained his feelings and motivations at the time of the betrayal. This is what was going on inside of him. These are the things that made him vulnerable to temptation."

"It sounds more like excuses to me," she said.

"You see?" said Robert. "I can't win!"

This was a difficult session for Robert and Joyce. Robert found it difficult to be honest about his feelings at the time of his transgression. Joyce struggled with an intense desire to know what was going on inside of him and a deep fear of hearing the answers. They were both defensive and easily slipped back and forth from honesty to blame.

Robert finally said, "I'm getting exhausted. She keeps asking me the same question five or ten times. I start changing my answers because I guess I'm not saying the right things. Nothing I do makes her stop."

"Your goal is not to make her stop," said Andy. "Your goal is to help her see that you are willing to do whatever it takes to help her heal—even if it means answering the same questions many times. Remember, the answers are not enough without transparency. You must tell her what was going on in your life when these things were occurring. She will know if you are shutting her out. She will continue to probe. She will not be satisfied until she feels that you are completely transparent with her. If she senses you are hiding something, she will not heal toward your marriage."

"But I don't always know the answers."

"That's OK. Answers are not nearly as important as transparency. Some questions do not have answers, but you can always describe the feelings and circumstances that you experienced at the time of the betrayal. Even if you cannot explain them, you can describe them." Andy could see that Robert needed a more thorough explanation, but he feared that a detailed discussion would cause Joyce further unnecessary pain. So, he asked her to step out and relax in the waiting area while he and Robert continued.[32]

"I don't know if I can do this."

Andy smiled sympathetically. "Yes," he said. "I am asking you to do a difficult thing. Transparency can be frightening. It takes courage to be vulnerable."

"I feel like I'm doing penance. Like you are asking me to do something that is not me."

"Quite the opposite, Robert. I'm asking you to do something that will cause you to be more authentic."

"What do you mean?"

"That's what transparency is. It is the willingness to reveal your inner person to yourself and to your wife."

"But I am a private person."

"There is nothing wrong with that Robert. I am not asking you to stop being a private person. I am asking you to be a vulnerable husband. There is a difference."

"Why do I have to be vulnerable? Because I sinned? Is this my punishment?"

"No, in fact, it's the other way around."

"Huh?"

"Robert, you do not need to be vulnerable because you have sinned. You sinned because you have not been vulnerable."

"Now, I'm really confused."

"Robert, your unwillingness to open your heart to your wife is part of how you set yourself up to be tempted into adultery."

Robert looked confused. Andy continued, "Transparency between husband and wife is a crucial ingredient to a healthy marriage. You stated earlier that you are a private person. But think about it. Being a private person and committing adultery are contradictory. You took your privacy and shared it with someone other than your wife. You took intimacy and gave it away. That was not an act of privacy. Instead of giving emotional intimacy to your wife, you sought intimacy somewhere else. It all goes back to what we talked about before, when we talked about the lie of adultery."

"So you are saying that I was searching for intimacy all along. I thought that the relationship with Teresa would satisfy that for me, but it didn't. I should have been searching for it in my relationship with Joyce."

"Exactly. Robert, you can be a private person in general, and still be an intimate husband with your wife. It is because you closed yourself off from your wife that you were tempted into sin. Marriage is a process of becoming one with your wife. You cannot be united if you are not open. The sexual union is intended to be an expression of the emotional and spiritual union that is shared between a husband and wife. Think about it. Adam and Eve were naked and unashamed in the Garden until sin entered their relationship. It was when sin entered that they became uneasy with their nudity. Yet it was not sinful for them to be nude with one another. Why do you think they were suddenly ashamed of their nudity?"[33]

"Because they had sinned. I think I get it. There was something wrong with them inwardly, so that became a problem with them physically."

"Right! Our spirit and our flesh are not completely separate entities. In marriage, what occurs relationally between a man, his wife, and God will immediately affect the sexual relationship, as well. They are interconnected. When you ostracized yourself from Joyce by shutting her out of your spirit, you separated yourself from her sexually, as well. Instead of working on your relationship with Joyce, you sought to satisfy yourself elsewhere. And for a short time, you thought you had been satisfied. But it was only an illusion. What you were really seeking was the kind of emotional and spiritual intimacy that God designed for marriage. In order to accomplish this, you and Joyce need to learn to communicate honestly at a deeper level than you are accustomed to."

"But you are asking me to start now, when Joyce is so angry. I feel like you are asking me to walk into a minefield!"

"It will be difficult at first, Robert. It takes practice. And you are right. You are going to be learning transparency at a difficult time. God's plan was that you learn it sooner. When God instructed husbands to love their wives as Christ loved the church, He explained that men are to follow Christ's example of giving Himself for the church.[34] Men often think, *Well, Christ died for the church, so if I ever have to, I'll be willing to throw myself in front of a bullet to save my wife's life.* But Christ gave Himself for the church in many other ways before He gave the ultimate gift of His life on the cross. He gave up His throne in heaven, His status. He gave up the security of a quiet carpenter's life. He traveled from place to place teaching and demonstrating Himself as the revelation of God. He didn't just pop up one day and say, 'OK, I'm here to be the hero. I'll take the bullet.' There was much more involved. Part of the purpose of Christ's coming was the revelation of God and the revelation of God's kingdom. This is the role that husbands are to take in their relationships with their wives. When you reveal your inner being to your wife, you are following Christ's example of revelation. This is what Christ did for the church. The good news is that you don't do this alone because God is involved. The power comes from Him. You have committed yourself to do this with the help of the Lord. He knows you better than you know yourself, and He will help you learn to be transparent. You have also established a support system with your pastor and friends at church. And if you ever come up against a problem that seems unsolvable, you can always bring it to a counseling session. We can sift through it together. Look at it this way, if you can learn to be transparent with the issue of your affair, you will be a pro at it by the time you and Joyce have rebuilt your marriage. In the future, being transparent about everyday issues will be much easier for you."

"Yeah, I guess you have a point. But it's not going to be easy."

"Let's pray together, Robert. We'll ask the Lord to strengthen you for the task ahead."[35]

Just as two spouses have needs that differ in relation to replacing support versus running for cover, so also do they have differing needs concerning seeking for answers and searching for an end. This set of different needs comprises the final movement of our dance. The offender's deepest desire is to be rid of shame and hurt. They want to forget the issue and bring the reconciliation process to an end. But the spouse who has been betrayed has many questions that must first be answered. Shock, anger, and grief have damaged the relationship. Trust and security need to be rebuilt.

In our story, Robert could have tried to make Joyce feel as though his decisions were her fault. This is why counseling with a Christian therapist is so important when reconciling after infidelity. Few people can go through this excruciating phase of self-examination and questioning without an impartial mediator to help guide them through it.

Often the wounded spouse feels as though they have been thrust into the midst of a complicated puzzle whose pieces do not fit together. There is sometimes a strong feeling that no sense of stability can be found and no forgiveness can be given unless the pieces are put together and the puzzle is complete.

Once again, the offender is called upon to lay aside their own needs in favor of helping the wounded spouse to heal. This movement in their dance is vital for rebuilding trust. The betrayed spouse must come to a sense of understanding about what happened. This understanding will come only if their questions are answered. Although the task may seem enormous for the repentant spouse, it is helpful to keep two things in mind. First, as with the other stages of restoring the marriage, this phase is temporary. Given the freedom to progress in their own time frame, the wounded spouse will eventually move beyond a need to ask these questions.

Second, this period of questioning is a pathway toward obtaining something the repentant spouse deeply desires: understanding. Although the therapeutic process does not seek to excuse an offender for the choice of infidelity, it does recognize that the offender has a side to the story, as well. There were ingredients in the marriage, in their life, and in their character, that caused vulnerability to temptation. The decision was wrong, sinful, and inexcusable. But the mind-set and emotional makeup at the time of the betrayal can be understood. Giving patient, honest answers to the wounded spouse's questions will bring understanding as an eventual by-product of the process.

Robert wanted to make the questioning process go away. As Andy pointed out, the goal is not to avoid the questions, but to help one's mate get through this process. How? The answer is simple but not easy. The questions need to be answered. The difficulty lies in answering them honestly, consistently, and transparently.

Honesty. It is important to tell the truth. When one person has lost faith in another, the only way to rebuild trust is to be honest. This means that the repentant spouse must be honest with self and with God.

Consistency. Often a person will become frustrated with the spouse's repeated questions. A question is asked. It is answered. Then it is asked again. The repentant spouse begins to think, *Well, the last answer didn't satisfy. Maybe if I change my answer, the question will go away.*

But the goal is not to make the questions go away. It is to promote healing and understanding. This can only be done with the truth. If two different answers are given to the same question, the wounded spouse will become confused. Trust will not be given. Instead of evading, avoiding, or changing answers to questions, telling the truth is paramount. If the questions are repeated, then the truth needs to be repeated, too.

On the other hand, it is appropriate to expand the answers. If the question is, "Why did you have the affair?" the answer might be, "I was feeling depressed." Later, the same question may appear. "But why did you have the affair?" The same answer can be given, but in expanded form. For example, a person might say, "Well, I was pretty depressed. I had just lost that big account that the firm was counting on, and our youngest daughter had just gone off to college. I wasn't where I thought I should be in this stage of my life, and I was getting bored and depressed." In this manner, the answer is consistent, but more information is given.

Transparency. This is usually the most difficult portion of the questioning phase for the repentant spouse. Transparency and vulnerability are ingredients that can cause much insecurity. Often, these ingredients were missing from the marriage before the infidelity. Learning to develop them while in the volatile process of restoration can seem overwhelming. However, if this is done faithfully, progress will be made toward healing the spirit of the wounded spouse, and the repentant spouse will make progress in becoming a transparent marriage partner. This growth will serve them both well throughout the rest of their marriage.

At this point, it is necessary to point out some areas of caution. Not all questions are healthy questions for the victim to ask. Any inquiry that has to do with sexual comparison is not recommended because it has no healing quality. Questions such as, "Which one of us is better in bed?" or, "What kind of sex did you have?" will haunt the wounded spouse for a long time. There is no benefit to be received from the answers.

On the other hand, almost anything else is a fair question that will help foster healing. Some questions like these might be:

"On February 2nd, you were three hours late. You said you were working. Were you with her (him)?"

"Did you take her (him) with you on your trip to Dallas?"

"Had the affair already started when we went out with her (his) family on her (his) birthday?"

"How many times did the two of you have sex?"

These are appropriate questions that should be answered. To an extent, this is a legitimate need. If it is not met, healing toward the marriage will be obstructed. That is why the question-and-answer process is important. However, the level of anger can be high within the victim, and feelings can be intense. In therapy, the counselor should diffuse the emotional intensity. Few couples can endure this phase without the help of an impartial "referee" such as Andy.

The process of questioning and answering between Joyce and Robert went on for quite some time. For a while, it didn't seem like the couple was making any progress. One day Robert asked Andy, "When are you going to challenge her to forgive me? Sometimes she is so angry."

"I want to forgive Robert," said Joyce. "I know that I need to do that, but I feel like I am trying to solve a puzzle. There are lots of loose pieces that are thrown about in my life. Unless I can find the pieces and put them together in a sensible manner, I don't think I can get over this."

"Robert, one of the reasons that the process of transparency is required is that Joyce needs expression and venting in order to heal. If her questions remain trapped, then resentment, anger, hostility, and frustration will develop and impede her healing."

"But when will it all end?"

"It takes time, Robert. And the time frame is different for each person."

"I'm just getting so tired."

"Well, that's understandable. This is a difficult process. Joyce, how do you feel things are going?"

"Sometimes I think it is going well. I have to give Robert credit. I can see that he really is trying. But sometimes I wonder if I'm ever going to feel secure in our marriage again. Sometimes I'm so angry I scare myself."

"Well, it's possible for you to get stuck in the anger. That's why it is so important for you to keep coming in and doing such a great job of being honest about your feelings. If I see that you are getting obsessed with your anger, you and I can work on that together, apart from Robert."

"I'm kind of relieved to hear you say that. I have been starting to get a little worried about the fact that I feel angry so much of the time."

"I'll tell you what, Joyce, when we are finished today, why don't we make next week's appointment for just you. We can explore your emotions and make sure you are still in the realm of healthy anger."

"That sounds like a good idea to me."

Andy reached for his Bible. "I want to read a passage of Scripture to you both. Romans 8:28–30 says, 'And we know that all things work together for good to those who love God, to those who are the called according to His purpose. For whom He foreknew, he also predestined to be conformed to the image of His Son, that He might be the firstborn among many brethren. Moreover whom He predestined, these He also called; whom He called, these He also justified; and whom He justified, these He also glorified.' Both of you have received Christ as your personal Savior. That means that you have been called according to the purpose of God. And what is His purpose for you? Primarily that you be conformed to the image of His Son. Marriage is a tool that He uses to help conform us to be more like Jesus. He wants to accomplish this in both of your lives as individuals. And He wants to accomplish this in you as a union. It is His desire to use a healthy, vibrant marriage as a tool to accomplish this in your life. But He is gracious. He will use this difficult period of your life as well. He will use it to accomplish His work in both of your lives."

Andy shifted his focus back to Robert. "Another reason the questions are necessary is for the process of repentance. Robert, you have expressed sorrow for your decision to cheat on Joyce. I remember what a step of courage it was for you to ask her to forgive you."

"Yeah, she said that she forgave me. But sometimes I wonder if she really did."

"Joyce, did you mean it when you told Robert that you forgave him?"

"I thought I did. I wanted to, but I had no idea how hard things were going to get."

"That's well put and it's the heart of what is occurring between you and Robert right now. You were telling Robert the truth when you forgave him, but that was before the reality of your emotional pain became so strong. Neither of you realized the enormity of the task that lay before you, primarily because neither of you realized the depth of the infraction that betrayal is to a marriage. Joyce, as you express your feelings, you realize how deeply you have been hurt. Robert, as you attempt to become transparent and allow her to express her hurt, you become aware of the level of her pain."

"So, she's not exaggerating."

"Right."

"But what does this have to do with repentance? I've already done that."

"Well, you have asked for Joyce's forgiveness. But, as you have just said, you really weren't aware of what you were asking at the time. You didn't know how much you were asking Joyce to forgive. In order for sinners—all of us, not only those who commit adultery—to fully repent of sin and move toward godliness, it is helpful that we understand the enormity of our sin. Sometimes the sinner is allowed to escape facing his sin. This is an injustice to him because he will not be able to fully repent. In the case of infidelity, this is one sin that specifically carries with it self-centeredness. For a person to come out of self-centeredness, it is necessary to focus on the hurt and pain they have caused in another person. If you are to grow to hate the sin and thereby resolve to never commit that sin again, the pain of introspection and of working to understand and feel Joyce's hurt is required."

"Feel her pain? Isn't that penance?" asked Robert.

"No. This is accepting the blame. Penance is attempting to do something to try to make up for or undo what has been done. It is an attempt to earn forgiveness. Forgiveness is a gift from God and a gift from your wife. It cannot be earned. But the restoration of your relationship requires full repentance. Full repentance requires understanding of the severity of the sin."

Robert did not like this explanation. He was beginning to feel the weight of the pain he had brought into the relationship. However, to his credit, he chose to continue trying to grow. As the weeks passed, he began to realize how important this process of repentance was for helping to reestablish Joyce's trust.

As couples enter the process of restoration, they are often unaware of the enormity of the damage that has been done to the marriage. As the layers of anger are slowly peeled away, the depth of the infraction becomes more apparent. The act of adultery usually involves at least three levels of offense. First, there is an emotional movement away from the spouse and toward the adulterous partner. The marriage relationship suffers a depletion of nurture and growth, because the nurture and growth that rightly belonged to the marriage is given to the adulterous relationship. Second, there is the damage caused by the denial of the affair. Because the adulterer has invested in two relationships, they believe that both must be maintained in order to achieve happiness. To keep the affair from being discovered, thus jeopardizing both relationships, an elaborate denial is begun when confrontation occurs. To hide guilt, intentional demeaning and blaming take place. This results in a great loss of self-worth and dignity on the part of the faithful spouse. Finally, there is the act of adultery itself. This is an act of betrayal. It is devastating to the wounded spouse, and it is damaging to the adulterer, as well. Therefore, not only does the betrayer injure the marriage, but they also return to the relationship in a used and spoiled condition themselves. This is why the dance of restoration is a complex process, requiring much time and patience before trust can be restored to the relationship.

Rebuilding the Marriage

Trust, Love, and Affection

By this time, Robert and Joyce had come a long way in restoring their marital relationship. Robert still wearied of Joyce's questions, but he had decided to be persistent and answer them as well as he could. It was not easy, but he knew it was necessary. After a while, he began to see positive changes in Joyce and to have hope for their relationship. But in their next session, he expressed a new concern.

"I am beginning to see how deeply I have hurt Joyce and how much pain my affair has caused her. It has really been tough to let her express all of her anger toward me and to try to answer all of her questions. But I believe that all of this is strengthening our relationship. Besides, seeing her pain is creating compassion in me for her. I seem to love her more. I never really knew how to talk to Joyce on an emotional level in the past. But just when I start to have hope that this is all going to work out, things start to unravel."

"What do you mean?" asked Andy.

"It's trust," said Joyce. "I don't trust him anymore. I want to. I'm still angry with Robert, but I can see that he is trying to make this marriage work. We have communicated more in these past few months than we have in our entire marriage. But that's part of the problem. I have always wanted to have this kind of communication. I resent that it took an affair to bring us to this point. Every time I start to think I can trust Robert, and I start to feel close to him, I remember what sparked all of this growth. And I hate it. I can't seem to get past the fact that he has had an affair. Then he gets frustrated with me for pulling back, and I stop believing him completely. When he pressures me to trust him or get close to him, I feel as if we are playing a game. It seems he is going through all of the motions just to win the game. I stop believing everything he says, and the cycle starts all over again."

"Wow!" said Andy. "Would you two think about the level of honesty you just expressed? Both of you shared your honest frustrations without attacking each other. You are really making progress!"

Robert and Joyce looked at each other in surprise. "Are you trying to tell us that this is a *good* problem?" asked Joyce.

Andy smiled. "I am telling you that you are progressing. You are both expressing yourselves clearly and in a healthy manner. You are trying to understand each other without defending or denying your own feelings. A lot can be done to heal a relationship when a couple reaches this point."

"Well, I guess that's good news," said Robert tentatively.

"I have more good news for you. What you are experiencing is normal. Most couples seeking restoration from infidelity reach this same juncture—that is, if they make it this far. You two really have a chance to build a solid marriage if you will continue to work as you have." Joyce and Robert looked relieved. Eventually they would be able to testify to the truth of Andy's words.

As Robert allowed Joyce to ask all of her questions, he answered them over and over again. He was diligent in his pursuit of transparency. It was hard work, but he maintained consistent, trustful behavior over a long period of time. Gradually, he rebuilt the ingredients of love, affection, and even trust in his wife. Much to her surprise, Joyce began to find the strength to encourage and accept his attempts to do this.

Betrayal robs the spouse of trust, love, and affection toward the one who cheated. Every move becomes suspect. At times, there is hatred toward the repentant spouse, and this usually causes guilt. The betrayed spouse often thinks that the loss of warm feelings is due to a personal failure. Sometimes friends and other well-meaning people insinuate that they are at fault for losing these feelings. The individual then works hard to rebuild trust and love. However, because the loss of these feelings came about through betrayal, the restoration must come about through love, faithfulness, and consistency on the part of the repentant spouse. It is not the task of the injured spouse to re-create these feelings, but the task of the betrayer to nurture them back to life in the spouse.

Over time, the wounded spouse needs to learn to acknowledge the consistency and faithfulness of their mate and even offer some encouragement. This is helpful to the process of restoration and will give hope to the couple. Even so, it is not wise to force these feelings into existence. It is best to allow the offending spouse to gradually show their faithfulness. Consistency, time, and trust in God can allow the betrayed spouse to relax and wait.

Another aspect to emotional healing is to enter into the miracle of forgiveness. The word *forgiveness* can arouse fright and anger in many people. However, under the leadership of the Holy Spirit and through His power, forgiveness can bless the couple and the marriage, and can also act as a soothing ointment to a raw and sensitive soul.

~

Forgiving the Spouse Who Strayed

One week Joyce was upset when she arrived for her appointment.

"Do you remember the friend I told you about? The one from my church? I have been confiding in her throughout this disaster."

"Yes. She has been a faithful prayer partner for you, hasn't she?"

"Well, yes, she has, but I'm really angry with her right now."

"Really? Why is that?"

"Well, she said that I need to forgive Robert for cheating on me. She said at some point I would need to obey God and forgive. I was surprised at the anger her words stirred in me."

"Have you forgiven Robert?"

Joyce seemed confused. "Well, I have told Robert that I forgive him, and I feel less and less angry as time goes by. But I'm not sure he really deserves my forgiveness. I mean, that is one reason I have liked coming to you. You haven't been cramming Bible verses down my throat."

Andy chuckled. "I'm glad you haven't felt pressured. And I do agree that Robert doesn't deserve your forgiveness. But do you really think that's the issue here?"

"I don't know what you mean."

"I didn't bring up the issue of forgiveness before now because you were in a great deal of pain."

"But you think I ought to forgive Robert."

"Well, yes. Those Bible verses about forgiveness shouldn't be, as you said, crammed down your throat. But they are the Word of God. They are truth. And truth brings life."

"And so it's my responsibility to bring life to Robert because he has repented."

"Well, yes and no. No, because ultimately it's God's responsibility to bring life to Robert. And yes, because God will use your forgiveness as a tool to give him life."

"But, God doesn't really need me, does He? He can use any tool He wants to bring life to Robert."

"Well, that's partly true. Robert can gain all the forgiveness he needs from God. But you worded your questions well. God can use any tool He wants. The truth is, He wants to use you."

"But why? That seems so unfair. I'm the one who was hurt."

"Yes. You've been hurt, and unfairly so. But one reason God wants to use you as a tool in Robert's life is because this will bring life to you, as well. Forgiveness is for the benefit of the one who forgives as much as it is for the benefit of the one who is forgiven."

"Now I'm really confused."

"God's truth brings life. Robert brought destruction to you. He brought death to the trust you had in him. He has done much to rebuild that, but he cannot bring life to your spirit. Only God can do that."

"OK, I'm listening."

"Betrayal. Loss of trust. We were not designed for these things. They plant hurt in our souls. If we allow the hurt to stay, if we nurture it and embrace it, we allow bitterness to take root. Bitterness will choke the life out of your spirit."

"So, I need to forgive Robert to keep the life growing in my spirit."

"Right. You are correct when you say that Robert does not deserve your forgiveness. None of us deserves to be forgiven. Your forgiveness will be an act of grace toward Robert. An undeserved gift. It will be an act of life for yourself and for your marriage."

"But I'm not sure I can do it."

"You have already shown yourself to be a person of great fortitude and strength. If someone had told you a year ago that you would be able to withstand this assault on your marriage, would you have believed them?"

"Well, no, I guess you're right. I never thought about that."

"A year ago, you didn't need the mercy of God to get you through these difficulties. God gave you the measure of grace and mercy you would need at each step of the way."

She paused to consider Andy's words. "Is that what it means when the Bible says that God will be strong in our weaknesses?"

"I think that is exactly what it means. You don't have the desire to forgive Robert within yourself. You see the damage he has done, and you rightfully assess that he doesn't deserve forgiveness. But God wants to use your act of forgiveness to bring healing to your inner being. Your task is to believe God and obey Him by forgiving Robert. Trust God that He is right, and then do it."

"That sounds good, but how do I do it?"

"First, you need to forgive Robert privately."

"Privately?"

"By this, I mean inwardly. Go to God and ask Him for His measure of forgiveness for Robert. Before God, decide to forgive Robert. Then, in prayer, declare him forgiven."

"Just like that? How will I know if I have fully forgiven Robert?"

"At first, you will just have to accept it based on faith. Do it because He said to do it and because you trust Him."

"But I don't think I can."

"God has given you every resource you need in order to forgive Robert."

"What do you mean?"

"When you received Christ as your Lord and personal Savior many years ago, the Holy Spirit came to live within you. Because you have the Holy Spirit inside of you, you don't need anything extra. You already have everything you need. You have God living within you."

"But I'm still so angry."

"Of course, you are! And you will be for a while. The act of forgiveness is a decision. It can happen in a moment, but the feelings associated with forgiveness come over time."

"So, it is possible for me to decide to forgive Robert even if I don't feel forgiving?"

"Right."

"Will I ever feel that way?"

"With consistency, over time, yes. I have a three-word model that can help you reach that point."

"OK, tell me about it."

"The first two steps I have already touched upon. *Decide* and *declare*. Decide to forgive Robert. Pray something like, 'Lord, I have decided to forgive Robert. I have decided to accept the miracle of forgiveness into my life.'"

"Then what?"

"Then you declare Robert forgiven."

"To Robert?"

"Not yet. Do this with God. Don't ask Him to help you forgive. Assume that God will do this through you. You can even declare that God will do this through you if you like."

"What do you mean?"

"I mean, go before God in prayer and declare Robert forgiven. Say something like, 'Lord, Robert has hurt me. He betrayed me, cheated on me, lied to me, and made me feel foolish. I now forgive him for all of these offenses. Because of Your strength in me, Robert is now completely forgiven by me. I turn him over to You for all the correction He needs. He is no longer my burden.'"

"That's it?"

"Well, life won't suddenly become easy. But a sincere prayer that seeks to rely on God's strength is all you need in order to accomplish forgiveness. It is complete at that point. But there will be more work to do in order to accomplish the *feeling* of forgiveness. That's where the third word comes in."

"Decide, declare, and what?"

"*Remind*. Many times you will remember the hurt Robert has caused you. The hurt will return. All your emotions will come back. You have already done much therapy to help recognize and express those emotions. Forgiveness can help to heal them."

"How?"

"Take them to God. Whenever you feel the negative emotions again, say something like, 'Heavenly Father, I forgave Robert and turned him over to You for correction. It is a finished matter. You are in charge. It is not my burden any longer.' A prayer such as this will continually keep in your mind the fact that you have forgiven Robert. It will move the burden off of you and onto God. It will accomplish the final processes of healing, and you will be free. Eventually, even the emotions will become less of a burden."

One mistake that Christians make when working with couples such as Robert and Joyce is to push toward forgiveness too early. One reason is that we often do not realize the depth of the pain that is present. This pain will surface in some form and cause further damage to the individual and to the marriage. We think, *Well, if you would just forgive, there would be no more pain.* But in reality, quick forgiveness is incomplete forgiveness, because the magnitude of the infraction must be fully realized before it can be fully forgiven.

Another reason we rush couples into forgiveness is that we haven't accepted the concept that the anger over infidelity is righteous anger and is in agreement with the character and nature of God. Finally, we often do not recognize that a person cannot forgive what they have not acknowledged. If the betrayed spouse has not had an adequate opportunity to verbalize the depth of pain inflicted by the perpetrator, it will not be possible to fully forgive. Later, the rest of the pain will surface in some form and cause further damage to the injured spouse and to the marriage. It robs the marriage of the full measure of forgiveness that is needed for restoration.

Once when Christ was visiting the home of a Pharisee, a woman with a bad reputation came into the house, anointed His feet with ointment, and washed them with her tears. In His explanation to the Pharisee, Jesus stated, "Therefore I say to you, her sins, which are many, are forgiven, for she loved much. But to whom little is forgiven, the same loves little" (Luke 7:47). This same concept can be applied to forgiveness in an adulterous situation. When the betrayed spouse recognizes and expresses the enormity of the pain inflicted, they are in a better position to offer total forgiveness. And when an adulterer repents of the full measure of the sin, with an understanding of the damage that was caused, it is then possible for them to fully love and rebuild love into the marriage.

While forgiveness should not be rushed, neither should it be withheld indefinitely. The concept of forgiveness is biblical and right. A wife or husband will not fully heal, either in the marital relationship or in relationship to God, if the miracle of forgiveness does not take place. There are several principles to keep in mind:

1. Forgiveness is not given because it is deserved. It cannot be earned. It is given by faith. The motivation does not come from the character qualities of the offender. It comes from a desire to experience the emotional and spiritual healing that only obedience to God can bring.

2. Forgiveness is a miracle that springs from the character of God. When we go to Him in prayer and declare another person forgiven, He agrees.

3. Forgiveness is not a feeling. It is a decision. Feelings follow as the healing process is worked out.

4. Forgiveness is not a process; healing is a process. Once forgiveness has been declared before God in prayer, it has taken place. It does not need to be repeated. It needs to be claimed or declared. When the angry or hurt feelings reoccur, they do not indicate a lack of forgiveness. They indicate that further healing still needs to take place. Part of the healing process is reminding oneself that these infractions have been forgiven. Answering the pain with a reminder will lessen the pain, and eventually it will be gone.

Sexual Relations in the Recuperating Marriage

Because the mind-set and physical makeup of a man is different from that of a woman, the sexual act requires different levels and types of commitment from each spouse. For the woman to have sex with her husband, she has to open herself to him. What he is doing is a physical intrusion to her. It is invasive. In order to have sex with her husband, she has to decide to become vulnerable to him. Thus, the physical union requires a depth of emotional involvement in order for her to fully enter into the act. She becomes both physically and emotionally open and moldable in order to receive him into her. This requires a great deal more trust for her than for him. Because he is the invader and she the invaded, she invests more emotionally into the sexual act. This investment is not necessarily required from him in order that he have a satisfactory experience. When the sexual act is over, she needs reassurance that her risk of vulnerability was well received. She needs reassurance of his love, faithfulness, and understanding of her gift. So, when a woman's trust has been violated, it is often necessary for that trust to be rebuilt in the marriage before she feels comfortable resuming sexual relations with her spouse. Often, her sexual desires will vacillate according to the state of her daily emotions.

For a man, the sexual act is its own reward. It in itself is an expression of his love. Through intercourse, he has succeeded in bonding, in expressing his love, and in receiving physical satisfaction, which can promote emotional satisfaction in him, as well. When a man engages in sex, he often experiences a sense of uniqueness. He feels special because he is the only one to whom his wife has granted sexual privilege. When a wife betrays a man, it is often this sense of exclusivity—and the security it brings—that is violated. Most men will react to this loss by sexually reasserting themselves in the marriage. Engaging in sexual relations temporarily helps them to reestablish the security that has been lost. As the wife continues to remain faithful and as the overall marriage is restored to health, the sense of security becomes more permanent.[36]

An affair shatters everything that has been built into the sexual relationship. This is one reason an affair is so devastating. Once this trust and bonding has been violated, much patience and hard work must be expended in order to rebuild a healthy and joyful sexual union.

One afternoon, several weeks after the couple began therapy, Joyce seemed to want to talk about something, but was hesitant to broach the subject. "I'm not sure how to ask this," she said. "But what about sex between Robert and me? I mean, I'm sure Robert has needs, but I don't always feel right about having sex with him. I'm afraid that if I don't, he'll go out and find his satisfaction somewhere else, but I resent having to think about that. I don't want to have sex with him just to keep him. Should I continue to engage in sex with him right now?"

"Most wives will at times be able to continue the sexual relationship, but at other times, they won't be able to," said

Andy. "You will go through periods when you want to have sex with Robert and other times when you don't. You should do what your feelings tell you that you are capable of doing. "And remember," Andy continued. "It is not your responsibility to keep Robert faithful. It is his responsibility to become a faithful person. So, don't worry about having sex with him in order to keep him from straying again. This will cause you to bear burdens that you are not intended to bear."

"In the meantime, what do I do?" asked Robert.

"The only thing you can do," replied Andy. "Leave it up to her. This is a good opportunity for you to deepen her level of trust in you. If you are understanding of her wavering emotions in this area, and if you are faithful to her in spite of the fact that you will feel some frustration, you will go a long way toward restoring Joyce's faith in you."

Later Andy and his intern, Suzannah Freeman, discussed the case together. "I noticed you encouraged Joyce to follow her feelings regarding the sexual relationship with Robert. Do you always counsel women in this way?"

"No," replied Andy. "Joyce is following a very typical pattern of reaction to an affair. Because of the level of trust that is violated, sometimes a wife cannot engage in sexual activity with her husband without images of the affair entering into her mind. As the two are having sex, the wife begins wondering what her husband did sexually with the other woman. She wonders if the other woman was better in bed. It is not wise to continue a sexual relationship at that time. Yet, the same woman can engage in the sexual relationship with her husband at other times without emotional and mental pain. It is normal for a woman to fluctuate between these two levels of trust while the marriage is recuperating."

"But this is not how all women respond?"

"No. People are different, and thus their reactions are different. I have found that women recuperating from their husbands' affairs react in three basic ways. Most women fluctuate in their desires, as Joyce described. Others want no sex at all with their husbands. They are disgusted and angry and do not want to be touched."

"And the third?"

"The third kind of reaction I see is that the woman actually becomes quite aggressive sexually."

"Aggressive?"

"Yes, some women desire sex more frequently with their mates. This type of woman sees sex as proof of his desire for her and as proof of his faithfulness. She gets upset if he doesn't show any interest, because she is using sex as a proof of her desirability. Often these women get facelifts, enter weight-loss programs, exercise excessively, and even have extensive cosmetic surgery. This is especially true if the husband has had an affair with a younger woman."

"How do you counsel a woman who is using sex as proof of her desirability?"

"I try to help her see that the driving force is not her actual need for sex, but her desire for her husband's approval. What she is using as proof is no proof at all. She believes a lie and needs to discard the lie."

"What do you mean?"

"A woman who is using sex as a proof of desirability is focusing on the wrong person. She is focusing on the other woman and competing with her. She needs to focus on God, herself, and her husband. Focusing on the other woman places her in a contest with falsehood. If she will focus on her relationship with God and grow in her discipleship, she will eventually find that she is sufficient and complete in Christ. If her husband will patiently and consistently build trust into her over time, she will learn that the sexual relationship is a gift God gave to each partner. This gift can be exchanged as an act of love and tenderness in the marriage bed for the sake of intimacy."

"What about the woman who wants no sex at all?"

Both of the extremes are a result of the wrong focus. But believe it or not, the woman who wants no sex at all is healthier than the woman who becomes aggressive."

"Really? Why is that?"

"Because she is reacting out of her normal emotions. She is operating in a normal reaction of anger, resentment, and a desire to make him pay. It is still a wrong focus, but it requires less work to fix."

"How do you address it?"

"Usually I just leave it alone and encourage her husband to be patient."

"You don't try to address it?"

"I will if it goes on for an extensive period of time, but that usually indicates that there is a sexual problem that is not related to the affair. Most of the time, as the woman goes through the healing process, her feelings of anger will subside. As the anger subsides, her resistance to sex subsides without outside interference. On the other hand, if she is pressured to have sex with her husband before she is ready, her anger will increase. Our goal is her healing. We don't want to create more hurt within her."

The sexual relationship is best when it is the result of intimacy. Sex will not create intimacy. Rather, intimacy will create satisfying, complete sex. Intimacy results from a nurturing relationship. It comes about in a marriage marked by spouses who uplift one another, bless one another, affirm one another, share with one another, minister to one another, pray for one another, face life's trials together, and engage in joint projects. Because an affair violates all of these things, it is natural that the sexual relationship will suffer. But it must be placed at a lower ranking order while the nurturing relationship is rebuilt. When intimacy is rebuilt into the relationship, a satisfying sexual relationship will usually be a natural by-product that will heal itself.

Falling in Love Again

When the affair is over, it is necessary to reconnect emotionally with the spouse. This may require great effort from the adulterous spouse. Sometimes these emotions have waned during the affair. Sometimes they seemed to disappear before the affair occurred, thus contributing to vulnerability in the area of temptation. When an individual has been convicted of sin and is now determined to repent and be faithful to God, they are then faced with an interesting dilemma: How can I enter into a fulfilling marriage relationship when I am no longer experiencing emotional love? Can I live a life of faithfulness, even though I believe the love is gone? This area of concern can become a major stumbling block in the process of rebuilding the marriage.

Fortunately, there is help for this dilemma. Application of the following principles will help the repentant spouse rediscover emotional love for their mate.

1. **Realize that the attraction to the adulterous lover is a lie.** What a person feels is not always the truth. The truth is what God says. The truth is what has been pledged and promised. An affair is the acting out of a blatant lie. No matter how good

it feels, the temporary happiness is a lie. Regardless of how exciting it might be, there is no truth to it. It is sin. Sin robs. Sin kills. It does not nurture or prosper. The truth is that an affair does not result in nurture or prosperity. The wife or husband is the one person that represents the best chance of happiness. Attempting to create an outside relationship will entangle all parties in many dire and negative consequences. It will never give freedom and completeness.

For a season, the attachment and sexual attraction toward the lover is new and different. It is strong. Nevertheless, it is a lie. Because of its strength, many people believe that it is the truth. They believe that it cannot be broken. But this is the truth: It can and must be broken in order to avoid disaster.

2. **Work is necessary to sever the tie to the lie.** The lie is severed through praying, thinking, speaking, and meditating upon the truth. All temptations to contact the other person must be resisted. Thoughts about the adulterous partner should be dismissed by using statements and prayers based on truth. For example, when the desire to continue the affair returns, pray something such as, "Father, this feeling is based upon a lie. I therefore reject it. I renounce it. I throw it away. I choose to turn from it. It is over. Thank You. Having this person in my life will not bring life—it will bring destruction. You have given me all I need in my own spouse. I choose to trust You to return my feelings for him (her). I choose to love my spouse. And today, before You, God, I declare that I love my spouse. I choose to live in faithfulness." Prayers such as this should be followed by an activity that will distract from unhealthy thoughts and feelings.

"How can I say these things if I do not feel them?" a person may ask. The issue is not prayer based upon feelings, but prayer based upon statements of truth and choice. The truth declares that emotions such as longing, need, or love for the other person are deceptions. Godly emotions will follow godly choices.

3. **The absence of emotional love for the spouse is the result of believing a lie.** Just as the emotions toward the other person are based on lies, so the absence of emotions toward the spouse is based on lies. It is true that the emotions are not present. That is an accurate assessment of the current feelings. However, feelings are fed by beliefs. In the case of pursing an outside relationship, the feelings were real, but they were fed by the lie that becoming involved with another person would meet genuine needs and bring satisfaction. In the same way, there are false beliefs that extinguish proper emotional feelings. In order for an individual to reestablish the emotional connection to their spouse, it is necessary to rebuild truth into the belief system.

Excitement, adventure, and pleasure are not love. They are enjoyable feelings, but they are not love. Love is commitment. Love has to do with choosing what is right in spite of feelings and apparent personal gain. When two people commit to each other in marriage—and that commitment is nurtured—the feelings of romance, love, and attraction will continue to grow. The love that God speaks of in Scripture is deeply intertwined with commitment and faithfulness. When these elements are deeply entrenched, the excitement, adventure, and pleasure will return to the marriage.

God has placed within each partner all of the love that will ever be needed. It may not be felt during an affair, but it is present. Commitment and faithfulness to these principles will eventually draw them out and bring an emotional celebration.

4. **Work is needed to unveil the love for the spouse.** Praying, speaking, and meditating upon the truth are vital actions

for recreating attraction. These mental activities then need to be followed by behavior that is conducive to the truth. For example, a repentant wife might spend thirty minutes a day talking to God (preferably out loud), saying something such as, "Heavenly Father, I love my husband. He is the one You gave to me. Therefore, he is Your perfect choice for me. Within his being resides all that I need to give me contentment and completion."

These prayers (which need to be prayed many times a day) should be followed with actions that express love. In his book *The Five Love Languages*, Gary Chapman gives excellent advice for helping marriage partners discover the love language of their mates. For example, one man might feel loved when his wife speaks words of admiration to him. In this case, an action that would express love would be for his wife to say, "I really admire the way you took time out to play with the children today." Or perhaps a woman feels loved when her husband enters into acts of service for her. So, he might choose to show her love by washing the dishes after dinner. When rebuilding the love relationship, it is important to rediscover actions and words that help each person to feel the emotion of love.

Another helpful tip is to return to some of the activities that were part of the dating and honeymoon period of the relationship. Was there a special restaurant? Was there breakfast in bed? Were flowers, cards, romantic e-mails, or gifts sent? Doing these things—even in the absence of loving or romantic feelings—can revive the emotions.[37]

Some people would say, "I don't feel these things. So I am being a hypocrite." But a hypocrite is a person who says one thing and does another. A hypocrite is a person who acts out a lie. We are proposing speaking and acting out a truth. Truth and feelings do not always coincide. Love between the husband and wife is still alive. That is the truth. The emotions say that love is gone. That is a lie. The love is not gone. The feelings of love have fallen asleep. They have been covered by sin. But God is merciful and has created us with the ability to restore these lost feelings. Speaking, acting out, and praying about the truth will revive them.

Romans 12:1–2 says "I beseech you therefore, brethren, by the mercies of God, that you present your bodies a living sacrifice, holy, acceptable to God, which is your reasonable service. And do not be conformed to this world, but be transformed by the renewing of your mind, that you may prove what is that good and acceptable and perfect will of God."

We are to throw ourselves upon the mercy of God. We sacrifice the unholy desires within us and replace them with what is holy and acceptable. We can be transformed by what our minds accept. If we simply follow our lusts, we are conformed to this world. But if we meditate on the truth, we will be transformed to what is holy and acceptable to God.

God does not leave us to stoicism. When we meditate upon what is good and acceptable unto Him, by His mercy, He transforms us completely to match the truth. Emotions are, to a large extent, the result of what is in our minds. Our beliefs, philosophies, thoughts, ideas, and words create our emotions. When we speak the truth, we are sending a direct message to our emotions. They will ultimately convert to what we are choosing to believe. If we practice behavior that is conducive to the truth we speak, we put our emotions in cross fire. We develop a philosophy, and we act upon it. The emotions then have no chance. They will eventually conform. It is not a matter of whether we feel the love initially. When we nurture it, it becomes an emotional reality. Our entire being will transform.

5. **Obedience to God must be established as the proper motivation for rebuilding the marriage relationship.** God's

Word gives instruction that genuine love is to be firmly entrenched in the marriage. Therefore, rebuilding the relationship is not an option for a person desiring to live a Christian life. We obey God because it is right, not because of a payoff we want to receive. We choose obedience, and if the rest of our life is spent in sacrifice in order to live out that obedience, this is the goodness of God working within us.[38]

6. **Over time, the preceding steps will reestablish the attraction and desire in the marriage.** Romans 6:8–23 speaks clearly to this concept. We are free to choose our bondage. Will we be bound to sin and to the things of this world, or will we bind ourselves to righteousness? Verse 11 gives this instruction: "Likewise you also, reckon yourselves to be dead indeed to sin, but alive to God in Christ Jesus our Lord." Verse 13 calls us not to yield ourselves as "instruments of unrighteousness to sin" but to yield ourselves to God as "instruments of righteousness." How are we able to do this? Verse 14 provides the answer: We are under the grace of God. God is faithful to us, and if we offer ourselves to Him as slaves to be used as instruments of righteousness, the benefits we will gain lead to holiness, and the result is eternal life.

God's truth leads to holiness and life. It leads to abundant life in this present world,[39] and to eternal life in the world hereafter.[40] God can take what we think is dead and make it alive again. He can take what we think was never there and create it. This is how we can say that if a person thinks, prays, meditates, and acts upon the truth, they will eventually feel the truth. God created emotions. They are intended for good. If sin, frustration, and daily living saturate these feelings, God's mercy can revive them. The requirement is an effort in trusting God. In the case of reestablishing emotions after an affair, the task is a laborious one that must be consistent over time. But the trust will come. Sexual attraction and excitement will return. Mental and emotional contentment will reestablish themselves, and something that is rather surprising will occur. The day will come when what is in faith being called a lie is clearly seen as what it is, a lie. The entire being will know this. Remorse for past actions will be experienced. The past behavior will be seen as foolishness. And the astonishing realization will come that there is physical, emotional, and spiritual rejoicing with the spouse.

"Blessed be the God and Father of our Lord Jesus Christ, who has blessed us with every spiritual blessing in the heavenly places in Christ" (Eph. 1:3).

Happily Ever After

Adultery is a lie. It involves exchanging God's truth for a lie. The book of Romans says that those who sin are without excuse, "because, although they knew God, they did not glorify Him as God, nor were thankful, but became futile in their thoughts, and their foolish hearts were darkened . . . who exchanged the truth of God for the lie, and worshiped and served the creature rather than the Creator, who is blessed forever. Amen" (Rom. 1:21, 25). Adultery is the act of serving the creature. It is self-gratification at the expense of others. Although it feels good in the beginning, the good feeling does not last.

The fact that sin feels good is no surprise to students of Scripture. Hebrews 11:25 says that Moses chose to suffer affliction along with the people of God rather than to enjoy the pleasures of sin for a short time. God does not say that sin is devoid of pleasure. He says that sin destroys. The book of Romans states that the wages of sin is death.[41] There is no escape from the destruction that sin brings. In the book of

Numbers, Moses warned the people of God, ". . . and be sure your sin will find you out" (Num. 32:23).

At first, the sin of adultery is gratifying. Life seems happier. But after a while, negative things begin to occur. Lovers begin to argue, and promises are broken. Clandestine visits become difficult, and keeping the secret becomes tiresome. Even though relating openly to each other is impossible, the secret meetings are no longer enough. Even the sex begins to lose the excitement it once had. Yet there is a reluctance to end the affair. Why?

The affair has levied a heavy price. The line of faithfulness has been crossed, and there is a need to somehow validate that decision. Consequently, the investment continues in the hope that the transgression will pay off. Life becomes a lie.

Living a lie is hard work. Much effort is made in an attempt to have a lie produce fruit that only the truth can yield. But no amount of energy can convert a lie into the truth. It is like living in a dark room and pretending to see. And with each day that passes, reality knocks louder and louder until it becomes a pounding nuisance that must be addressed, because truth is a visitor that will not go away.

There is a way out. But it is not an easy way. It involves repentance and living in truth. The adulterer must bear the weight of the destruction and accept the responsibility for rebuilding trust into the marriage. The injured spouse needs freedom to unleash the hurt, and the repentant spouse needs to take responsibility for soothing that hurt through humility and consistency. Even so, God is merciful.

Our heavenly Father does not want His children to hurt themselves. He desires to see husbands and wives walk in joy and beauty. He designed marriage to be a picture of the relationship of Christ and His church, and He longs to see that lived out in each union. As a couple submits to God and His ways, as they look to Him for their joy and satisfaction, He can bring reconciliation. He is the Great Reconciler.

It is our sincere hope that reading this book has been beneficial to your marriage. But we know that reading a book will not in and of itself bring about healing. Reading a book takes a few hours, but true restoration takes months and years of steady, unswerving hard work. We hope our words have been encouraging to you, and we pray that you will have the courage and maintain the energy that is necessary to bring restoration.

Through our years of working with people, one thing has become clear: Only God can heal the spirit. Much of what needs to occur for restoration to take place can only be brought about as the Holy Spirit works His mighty plan in each spouse. If infidelity has occurred, only God's hand can bring about repentance and true change in the inner being. If there has been wounding by betrayal, the miracle-working power of the Holy Spirit, who is also called the Comforter, can bring full healing and forgiveness and set a person free to experience the abundant life that He desires for every person. The principles laid out in this book can be an encouragement in appropriating the work of the Holy Spirit in each life, but only He can bring about the real change and healing that are necessary.

For this reason, there is one final, yet most important issue to address. Have you ever come to the place in your life that you have received Jesus Christ as your Lord and personal Savior? Have you surrendered yourself to Him and asked Him to make His desires the primary desires of your life? If not, we ask you to prayerfully consider doing so now. It is only by accepting Jesus Christ as your Lord and Savior that the Holy

Spirit's power can be born into your life. Read and carefully consider the following principles:

1. John 3:16 says, "For God so loved the world that He gave His only begotten Son, that whoever believes in Him should not perish but have everlasting life." God loves you. This love is not based upon your worth or value, but upon His loving nature. Because He desires to have a relationship with you, He made the ultimate sacrifice by giving His Son to die on the cross as a sacrifice for your sin.

2. Romans 3:23 says, "For all have sinned and fall short of the glory of God." Regardless of the circumstances that brought you to this book, Scripture teaches that all persons are sinful. It is sin that separates us from God.

3. Romans 6:23 says, "For the wages of sin is death, but the gift of God is eternal life in Christ Jesus our Lord." Because we are sinners, we are separated from the Life-Giver. This separation results in death. We experience spiritual death in this life, and reap the results of this death in our relationships, our bodies, and ultimately in our spirits after we die. Yet God desires to give us abundant life, both now as we live with Him on earth, and in heaven as we experience His glorious presence in eternity.

4. First John 1:9 says, "If we confess our sins, He is faithful and just to forgive us our sins and to cleanse us from all unrighteousness." If you desire to be born into the kingdom of God today, tell God that is what you desire. Ask Him to cleanse you of your sinfulness and to give you new life in Him.

If you have made a decision for Christ, we encourage you to seek out a pastor or trusted Christian friend as soon as possible and share your decision. This person will help you to understand important principles concerning following God through baptism, Scripture reading, church attendance, and discipleship. May God bless you and your spouse as you grow in Christ together.

> Now to Him who is able to keep you from stumbling,
> And to present you faultless
> Before the presence of His glory with exceeding joy,
> To God our Savior,
> Who alone is wise,
> Be glory and majesty,
> Dominion and power,
> Both now and forever. Amen.
>
> —JUDE 24, 25

Notes

1. This is especially true when the cheating spouse is the husband. Because women are usually more sensitive to the subtleties present in relationships, they tend to develop an early awareness that something is wrong in the marriage. Husbands are more likely than wives to be surprised when the unfaithfulness of their spouse is revealed. This is not always the case, however. Some men are highly alert to relationship nuances. In addition, some spouses are especially adept at deception, and their faithful spouses do not know anything is amiss for a long time, if ever, regardless of their gender. In these cases, usually discovery will occur only when there is a confession.

2. Other adulterers opt for passivity as their form of denial. They ignore the questions and refuse to discuss the issue.

3. "Let the husband render to his wife the affection due her, and likewise also the wife to her husband. The wife does not have authority over her own body, but the husband does. And likewise the husband does not have authority over his own body, but the wife does" (1 Cor. 7:3–4).

4. There are exceptions to this. Some people who commit adultery are not attempting to invest in other relationships and are not

necessarily displeased with their marriages. There are individuals who are motivated by the excitement and adventure of sexual liaisons and by an extreme level of self-centeredness. Some of these people could be labeled "sexual addicts."

5. Matthew 19:6. Some people even use this kind of thinking to justify an affair if their wedding wasn't "holy" enough. "We didn't get married in God's sight," they may say, "because we were married by a justice of the peace and not in the church." However, this kind of thinking represents an image of a limited God who only sees things that happen in church and who is capable only of holding people accountable to wedding vows that were made under ideal circumstances. Reality is quite the opposite. God is omnipresent. This means that He is present in all places at all times. Therefore, vows taken in the office of a justice of the peace are seen by Him as clearly as those taken in a church sanctuary.

6. There are a number of reasons why a person might do this. At times they are trying to manipulate their adulterous lover into a more committed relationship. They may be overwhelmed by their own guilt, or they could simply be cruel and want to brag. Often they include information that is not true, such as claiming that the unfaithful spouse is planning a divorce.

7. A possible exception to this is when the adulterer has decided to leave the marriage. In this case, they are more likely to admit to the affair for the sole purpose of bringing the marriage to a close. Sometimes this is done viciously.

8. It is important that counselors and pastors provide an atmosphere that encourages individuals to freely express themselves but also provides safety for those who might hear what is said. People in emotional pain are not tactful. They say injurious things that can further damage the relationship. Also, the spouse who has cheated needs to deal with issues (such as missing the adulterous partner) that might cause unnecessary hurt to the innocent spouse.

9. "You have heard that it was said to those of old, 'You shall not commit adultery.' But I say to you that whoever looks at a woman to lust for her has already committed adultery with her in his heart. If your right eye causes you to sin, pluck it out and cast it from you; for it is more profitable for you that one of your members perish, than

for your whole body to be cast into hell. And if your right hand causes you to sin, cut it off and cast it from you; for it is more profitable for you that one of your members perish, than for your whole body to be cast into hell" (Matt. 5:27–30).

10. For more about questions and answers, see chapter 5.

11. The only exceptions to this list are questions pertaining to sexual comparisons and sexual details. This information should not be lied about, but it should be answered with a response such as, "Let's wait and talk to our counselor about that one."

12. "Let no one say when he is tempted, 'I am tempted by God'; for God cannot be tempted by evil, nor does He Himself tempt anyone. But each one is tempted when he is drawn away by his own desires and enticed. Then, when desire has conceived, it gives birth to sin; and sin, when it is full-grown, brings forth death" (James 1:13–15).

13. Perhaps further therapy will expose why the desire to feel needed provided a strong temptation to sin.

14. "Husbands, love your wives, just as Christ also loved the church and gave Himself for her, that He might sanctify and cleanse her with the washing of water by the word, that He might present her to Himself a glorious church, not having spot or wrinkle or any such thing, but that she should be holy and without blemish. So husbands ought to love their own wives as their own bodies; he who loves his wife loves himself" (Eph. 5:25–28).

15. It is possible that some people might not encounter this desire to save the marriage. Most of these individuals do not choose to enter into the healing process. Others may choose to remain in the marriage because of religious conviction or concern for their children, even without experiencing an initial feeling of desperation. These people can still experience restoration as they continue to work through intense anger and the remaining movements in the process.

16. The way anger surfaces during this period will differ from person to person, depending upon their personalities and life experiences. However, the cycle Andy is describing is a common one seen in many clients, especially among women. Men, in general, tend to make slow, steady progress in dealing with their emotions, whereas women tend to be more cyclical. Regardless of the method of its

appearance, however, strong anger almost always surfaces during this period of the restoration process.

17. In order to illustrate the depth of pain on the part of the wounded spouse and the perpetrator's need to accept his or her mate's great anger, we have created a dialogue that contains the expression of harsh feelings. However, we want to caution counselors to prayerfully use their best judgment on this matter. On the one hand, clients, especially those who have been betrayed, need to be free to express strong feelings. This is an essential part of the healing process. On the other hand, the counselor may choose to separate the spouses for several sessions in order to minimize the damage that angry words can do to the relationship. The irony of the situation becomes apparent. Expression and acceptance of anger is necessary for healing and restoration, but many marriages cannot survive the level of anger that is present. Much prayer in seeking guidance and wisdom from God is needed.

18. This confusion is especially true when the husband has been the offending spouse. Men tend to be more straightforward and have a less complex emotional makeup than women. So when their wives return to anger, men tend to see this as illogical. Women are more accustomed to emotional upheavals. When women are the offenders, they may be surprised at their husbands' return to anger. But they are less bewildered and hopeless, because they are more accustomed to dealing with complex emotions.

19. "Wives, submit to your own husbands, as to the Lord. For the husband is head of the wife, as also Christ is head of the church; and He is the Savior of the body. Therefore, just as the church is subject to Christ, so let the wives be to their own husbands in everything . . . Nevertheless let each one of you in particular so love his own wife as himself, and let the wife see that she respects her husband" (Eph. 5:22–24, 33).

20. "Husbands, love your wives, just as Christ also loved the church and gave Himself for her; that He might sanctify and cleanse her with the washing of water by the word, that He might present her to Himself a glorious church, not having spot or wrinkle or any such thing, but that she should be holy and without blemish. So husbands ought to

love their own wives as their own bodies; he who loves his wife loves himself. For no one ever hated his own flesh, but nourishes and cherishes it, just as the Lord does the church" (Eph. 5:25–29).

21. "Husbands, likewise, dwell with them with understanding, giving honor to the wife, as to the weaker vessel, and as being heirs together of the grace of life, that your prayers may not be hindered" (1 Pet. 3:7).

22. In Hosea 6:1–11, the nation of Israel sought to treat their offenses lightly. God did not allow it.

23. See chapter 6 for more information on these issues.

24. We recommend that the wounded spouse stay away from the other party in all circumstances, and that over time forgiveness take place privately with God in his or her own heart. If a counselor is working with someone who insists on confronting the third person, the safest manner to do this is over the telephone. This will help dissuade violence should the confrontation turn intense.

25. These skills may be learned later, but they are not a focus at this stage of the restoration process.

26. This may need to be explored more thoroughly if the offender has never received Christ as Savior. For more information, see chapter 7.

27. See Proverbs 27:17

28. Note to ministers: It is vitally important that confidentiality be respected. If a couple is attempting to rebuild their marriage, publicity will only make that task more difficult. If a person is repentant and attempting to rebuild trust, they will need both support and privacy.

29. Many men, and some very private women, may not acknowledge this need due to embarrassment about the failure of the marriage. However, even those individuals who do not express a desire to talk do experience a barrage of strong emotions. A support system is still essential and should be developed, even if it is rather small.

30. Galatians 6:2

31. "Brethren, I do not count myself to have apprehended; but one thing I do, forgetting those things which are behind and reaching forward to those things which are ahead, I press toward the goal for the prize of the upward call of God in Christ Jesus" (Phil. 3:13–14).

32. In order to explain the concept of transparency, a counselor may need to initiate discussion about the affair. The perpetrator needs to understand that their transparency and intimacy has been given to the wrong person and needs to be transferred back to the spouse. However, it is not necessary for the wounded spouse to be subjugated to this kind of open talk about the adultery. Here, Andy has allowed Joyce to stay long enough to validate her need to ask questions and receive honest answers. Then he protects her from the discussion that will follow.

33. "Therefore a man shall leave his father and mother and be joined to his wife, and they shall become one flesh. And they were both naked, the man and his wife, and were not ashamed. . . . Then the Lord God called to Adam and said to him, 'Where are you?' So he said, 'I heard Your voice in the garden, and I was afraid because I was naked; and I hid myself.' And He said, 'Who told you that you were naked? Have you eaten from the tree of which I commanded you that you should not eat?' " (Gen. 2:24, 25; 3:9, 10).

34. See Ephesians 5:23–31.

35. In a real counseling situation, it would be wise to invite Joyce back to the session for the prayer time. If time allows, having Robert practice giving honest answers to some questions from Joyce would be helpful to Robert and would provide further validation for Joyce.

36. There are some men who experience a high level of emotional connection as a part of their sexuality. These men may experience the same wounds and vacillations that are described in the paragraph about a woman's reaction. When this is the case, the same advice given to the women applies to these men.

37. For more information on practical ways to express love to your spouse in their love language, see the book *The Five Love Languages* by Gary Chapman, published by Moody.

38. "For this is commendable, if because of conscience toward God one endures grief, suffering wrongfully. For what credit is it if, when you are beaten for your faults, you take it patiently? But when you do good and suffer, if you take it patiently, this is commendable before God. For to this you were called, because Christ also suffered for us, leaving us an example, that you should follow His steps: 'Who committed no sin, nor was deceit found in His mouth'; who, when He was

reviled, did not revile in return; when He suffered, He did not threaten, but committed Himself to Him who judges righteously; who Himself bore our sins in His own body on the tree, that we, having died to sins, might live for righteousness—by whose stripes you were healed. For you were like sheep going astray, but have now returned to the Shepherd and Overseer of your souls. . . . But even if you should suffer for righteousness' sake, you are blessed. 'And do not be afraid of their threats, nor be troubled.' But sanctify the Lord God in your hearts, and always be ready to give a defense to everyone who asks you a reason for the hope that is in you, with meekness and fear; having a good conscience, that when they defame you as evildoers, those who revile your good conduct in Christ may be ashamed. For it is better, if it is the will of God, to suffer for doing good than for doing evil. For Christ also suffered once for sins, the just for the unjust, that He might bring us to God, being put to death in the flesh but made alive by the Spirit" (1 Pet. 2:19–25, 3:14–18).

39. "The thief does not come except to steal, and to kill, and to destroy. I have come that they may have life, and that they may have it more abundantly" (John 10:10).

40. "But now having been set free from sin, and having become slaves of God, you have your fruit to holiness, and the end, everlasting life. For the wages of sin is death, but the gift of God is eternal life in Christ Jesus our Lord" (Rom. 6:22, 23).

41. "For the wages of sin is death, but the gift of God is eternal life in Christ Jesus our Lord" (Rom. 6:23).